Proceedings of the Boston Area Colloquium in Ancient Philosophy

Proceedings of the Boston Area Colloquium in Ancient Philosophy

VOLUME XXXIII

Edited by

Gary M. Gurtler, S.J.
William Wians

BRILL

LEIDEN | BOSTON

This paperback is also published in hardback under ISBN 978-90-04-37694-6.

Typeface for the Latin, Greek, and Cyrillic scripts: "Brill". See and download: brill.com/brill-typeface.

ISSN 1059-986X
ISBN 978-90-04-37693-9

Copyright 2018 by Koninklijke Brill NV, Leiden, The Netherlands.
Koninklijke Brill NV incorporates the imprints Brill, Brill Hes & De Graaf, Brill Nijhoff, Brill Rodopi,
Brill Sense and Hotei Publishing.
All rights reserved. No part of this publication may be reproduced, translated, stored in a retrieval system,
or transmitted in any form or by any means, electronic, mechanical, photocopying, recording or otherwise,
without prior written permission from the publisher.
Authorization to photocopy items for internal or personal use is granted by Koninklijke Brill NV provided
that the appropriate fees are paid directly to The Copyright Clearance Center, 222 Rosewood Drive,
Suite 910, Danvers, MA 01923, USA. Fees are subject to change.

This book is printed on acid-free paper and produced in a sustainable manner.

Contents

Preface VII
Notes on Contributors IX

COLLOQUIUM 1
Parmenides, Liars, and Mortal Incompleteness 1
Rose Cherubin
Commentary on Cherubin 22
Yale Weiss
Cherubin/Weiss Bibliography 27

COLLOQUIUM 2
The Metaphysics of the Syllogism 31
Edward C. Halper
Commentary on Halper 61
Owen Goldin
Halper/Goldin Bibliography 68

COLLOQUIUM 3
Likely and Necessary: The *Poetics* of Aristotle and the Problem of Literary
Leeway 69
Jean Marc Narbonne
Commentary on Narbonne 88
J. Aultman-Moore
Narbonne/Aultman-Moore Bibliography 93

COLLOQUIUM 4
A Man of No Substance: The Philosopher in Plato's *Gorgias* 95
S. Montgomery Ewegen
Commentary on Ewegen 113
J.M. Forte
Ewegen/Forte Bibliography 118

Index 121

Preface

Volume 33 contains papers and commentaries presented to the Boston Area Colloquium in Ancient Philosophy during the academic year 2016–17. The Colloquia for this year includes papers on Parmenides, Plato and Aristotle, and the commentators added robust challenges to the presenters' theses in significant ways. The first paper examines the intriguing role of the goddess in Parmenides' *Poem* as recommending one thing and doing another, a sort of liar's paradox that nonetheless reveals the paradoxes involved in human inquiry. The comment pushes back with a question about the use of *doxa* in the argument of the paper. The second paper presents an equally intriguing account of the syllogism in Aristotle's *Posterior Analytics*, that it is not a mental entity, but has a counterpart in nature. This claim is crucial for indicating the difference between Aristotelian logic and contemporary approaches to logic. The comment in this instances supports the claim of the paper, but notes the centrality of language rather than the mind, reinforcing Aristotle's distinction from modern concerns. The third presentation continues the examination of Aristotle, but in the different context of the *Poetics*. The artist has a particular authorial freedom in constructing a story, not bound by what is or what should be, but by what might be, arguing from the role of the 'likely and necessary' in Aristotle's analysis of the nature of poetry. The comment notes that this claim of artistic creativity seems to emerge more from post-Kantian Romanticism than the pen of Aristotle. The fourth paper gives a point and counterpoint about the nature of philsophy in Plato's *Gorgias*. Callicles attacks philosophy as taking away one's *ousia*, making its practitioners inept and powerless. Socrates is then taken as agreeing with Callicles, but as arguing that such lack of power is precisely the condition for the pursuit of the truth and the good. The comment gives some substance, so to speak, to Socrates' stance by bringing in his discussion of death, a reversal of Callicles' attack and emphasizing Socrates' active attempt to persuade, if not Callicles, at least the others present for their conversation.

The papers and commentaries appear in the order they were given at the different meetings of the Boston Area Colloquium in Ancient Philosophy at one of the following participating institutions: Assumption College, Boston College, the College of the Holy Cross, and St. Anselm College. The dialogical character of the colloquia is partially preserved by publishing both paper and commentary from each of the meetings. In many cases these oral presentations have been extensively revised, not to mention expanded, by their authors in the light of subsequent discussions, and especially in response to critical comments from our external referees. For their generous assistance as referees,

I would like to thank the following scholars: David Bronstein, Daniel Graham, Peter Hanley, Robert Metcalf, and Marjolein Oele. At the end of the volume, together with the section 'About our Contributors,' readers will find a general index of names which was collated by our editorial assistant, Sean Driscoll.

In conclusion, I wish to thank my colleagues on the BACAP committee, whose voluntary service structures the reality to which these Proceedings stand at one remove. Furthermore, I am much indebted to William Wians, who continues to serve as co-editor. I would also like to thank our editorial assistant, Sean Driscoll, for his outstanding work in preparing the copy for this volume in the Philosophy Department at Boston College, and for his countless other efforts in assisting the editors and the contributors in the process of bringing the papers to finished form. Finally, I want to acknowledge the continued financial assistance provided by the administration at Boston College, whose support for this project has remained most generous over the years.

Gary Gurtler, S.J.
Boston College

Notes on Contributors

J. Aultman-Moore

is Professor of Philosophy at Waynesburg University. He was educated at Boston College and Loyola University of Chicago. His area of specialization is Ancient Greek Philosophy and Literature. In addition, he is interested in the history of the relation of science and religion and the thought of the contemporary philosopher Charles Taylor.

Rose Cherubin

is Associate Professor of Philosophy at George Mason University. She was educated at the School of Visual Arts and at the Graduate School and University Center of the City University of New York. Her research has focused on the Eleatic philosophers, Plato, Aristotle, and Alain Locke.

S. Montgomery Ewegen

received his Ph.D. at Boston College in 2011, and is currently Assistant Professor of Philosophy at Trinity College. He is author of *Plato's Cratylus: the Comedy of Language* (Indiana University Press, 2013). He is finishing his second book on Plato, as well as a translation of Martin Heidegger's *Heraklit* lectures.

Joseph M. Forte

is Tutor (full-time faculty) and Academic Administrator at Northeast Catholic College in Warner, NH, where he teaches epistemology, logic, the philosophy of St. Thomas Aquinas, Eastern philosophy, and ancient Greek literature, history, and philosophy. He defended his dissertation: "Turning the Whole Soul: Platonic Myths of the Afterlife and Their Psychagogic Function," in August 2016 at The Catholic University of America School of Philosophy. His most recent article is titled "Explaining Hope in Plato's *Philebus*" (IPQ 2016). His current research projects focus mainly on epistemology, psychology, and ethics, in Plato as well as modern thought.

Owen Goldin

is Professor of Philosophy at Marquette University. He was educated at St. John's College, University of Chicago, and the University of Texas at Austin. Most of his publications have been in the area of ancient philosophy. He is the author of *Explaining an Eclipse: Aristotle's Posterior Analytics 2: 1–10* and has translated some of the commentary on the *Posterior Analytics* attributed to Philoponus for the Ancient Commentators Series. He is currently at work showing how within the *Posterior Analytics* Aristotle builds on and responds to earlier models of explanation.

Edward C. Halper

is Distinguished Research Professor and Josiah Meigs Teaching Professor of Philosophy at the University of Georgia. He was educated at the University of Chicago (B.A.), Columbia (M.A.), and the University of Toronto (Ph.D.). Although much of his published work is in ancient philosophy, he has also published work on figures and issues from other periods and on metaphysics. A particular interest is the metaphysical status of such Aristotelian entities as the human good, an act of virtue, and a state. He is currently completing the final volume of a three-volume study, *One and Many in Aristotle's* Metaphysics.

Jean-Marc Narbonne

is Professor in ancient philosophy at Université Laval (Québec, Canada), holder of the Chair *Canada Research Chair in the Critical Spirit in Antiquity and the Emergence of Modernity* (2015–2022), director of the Partnership research project *Raison et Révélation : l'Héritage Critique de l'Antiquité* (2014–2021), director of the editing and French translation project of Plotinus' complete work for the Budé collection (Les Belles Lettres). He also published many works, e. g. *Antiquité Critique et Modernité. Essai sur le rôle de la pensée critique en Occident* (Les Belles Lettres, 2016), Plotin, *Oeuvres complètes*, t. I, 1, Introduction générale, *Traité 1 : Sur le Beau*, Introduction, traduction et notes par Jean-Marc Narbonne, avec la collaboration de Martin Achard, texte grec établi par Lorenzo Ferroni, (Les Belles Lettres, 2012) ; *Plotinus in Dialogue with the Gnostics* (Brill, 2011).

Yale Weiss

is a PhD student in Philosophy at the Graduate Center of the City University of New York. Previous work of his on ancient philosophy has been published in *Phronesis* and the *Philosophical Forum*. His research interests include logic (ancient, philosophical, and mathematical), ancient science, and the philosophy of mathematics.

COLLOQUIUM 1

Parmenides, Liars, and Mortal Incompleteness

Rose Cherubin
George Mason University

Abstract

On the road of inquiry that Parmenides' goddess recommends, one is to say and conceive that what-is is one, unmoving, continuous, ungenerated, undestroyed, complete, and undivided. Yet the goddess's arguments in favor of this road use negations, distinctions, divisions, and references to generation and destruction. The requisites of inquiry that she outlines are both defined on and at odds with other features that inquiry appears to require. This essay argues that the goddess's arguments manifest something like a liar paradox: She demonstrates on the basis of the opinions of mortals that mortals' opinions are flawed. If so, then the goddess's arguments do not establish that what-is is one and unchanging. What they show is that what inquiry and inference seem to require, given the opinions of mortals, is at odds with itself. To refer to what-is is to make *aletheia* impossible to reach. To be mortal, for Parmenides, is to journey through that incompleteness.

Keywords

Parmenides – *doxa* – paradox – *aletheia* – proem

Aristotle remarks at *Metaphysics* 983a11 and following that achieving wisdom, gaining knowledge of first causes and principles, would "in a way bring us to the opposite [situation] to that out of which we began our inquiries."[1] As one example of that kind of progress to the situation opposite to that from which we started, he mentions that one might initially be amazed (θαυμάζειν) at the incommensurability (ἀσυμμετρία) of the diagonal of a square with the side. But one would cease to be amazed at this—one would expect the incommensurability—once one had learned the causes in geometry.

---

1   All translations are my own.

© KONINKLIJKE BRILL NV, LEIDEN, 2018 | DOI 10.1163/22134417-00331P02

This is a remarkable example. For understanding causes in geometry opens up another question for the search for first causes and principles: how is it that space, or for that matter what-is generally, encompasses incommensurables? How can something that seems to have endpoints be unlimited or indefinite in length? Why are some things incommensurable; why does conceiving one thing as definite make another indefinite? In other words, can we get to Aristotle's "opposite situation" from here? Can we even conceive of what that would be like from here? Can we know the answer to *that*, from here? And if not, is it even justified to say that we have any idea of what "wisdom" would involve?

Aristotle was not the first to contemplate the question of "Can we get there from here?" *as* a question. Nor was he the first to uncover incommensurabilities and incompleteness when he explored the question. I would submit that Parmenides did it before him. Parmenides did not refer to a search for wisdom or for first causes, but he did explore something closely related. His poem poses the question of how to speak and conceive of what-is[2] in a way that accords with (and does not also conflict with) ἀλήθεια (roughly, the truth, the whole truth, and nothing but the truth, traced to its origins).[3] More, it poses the question of what inquiry, δίζησις, in accordance with ἀλήθεια would require. What would it take to speak and conceive of what-is in a way that accords with ἀλήθεια? Can we get there from here? What would it take to inquire in a way that is oriented by ἀλήθεια, to follow a road of inquiry associated with ἀλήθεια; and is that within the realm of possibility for us? Can we form a coherent account of how to do that, from here?

'Here,' in this case, is our everyday worldview, framed by our (mortals') opinions. 'There' would be ἀλήθεια, or at least something consonant and not also dissonant with it. Are mortal opinions even such as to enable us to conceive and speak of what-is in a way that conduces to ἀλήθεια? Are mortals' opinions in keeping and not also in conflict with what inquiry requires? Or is there some apparent incommensurability, so that we really cannot see how or whether we can get there from here?

To see how Parmenides posed these questions, how he explored them, and what he uncovered regarding them, let us start by looking at the structure of the extant fragments (section I). Next, we will turn to what this structure reveals about one of Parmenides' areas of focus: the attention Parmenides paid to what I will call the requisites of inquiry—or, more precisely, the requisites of inquiry given our starting-points (II). Then we will look at those starting-points,

---

2   To avoid phrases such as 'what is is,' I will use the hyphenated 'what-is' to translate Parmenides' 'ἐόν' or 'τὸ ἐόν.'

3   Cf. Krischer 1965; Levet 1976; Cole 1983, 8; Constantineau 1987; Germani 1988; Detienne 1990.

which I shall try to show reflect in important ways the opinions of mortals that the goddess describes (III). From there, we will examine how the goddess's speech about roads of inquiry relies on the opinions of mortals to challenge the opinions of mortals (IV); and we will try to take stock of some of the implications (V). Finally, we will consider the relationships that Parmenides' work seems to suggest between those opinions and being a mortal, that is, the relationship between mortality and incompleteness (VI).

I   The Extant Fragments of Parmenides: Structure

Sextus preserved what he reported to be the beginning of Parmenides' poem, a first-person tale of a young man's journey to the realm of a goddess (DK B1.1–30).[4] The goddess welcomes the narrator and declares that he is to learn both the "heart of ... ἀλήθεια/ and the opinions of mortals, in which there is no true assurance (πίστις ἀληθής)" (B1.29–30). The remaining fragments seem to be parts of the goddess's speech in fulfillment of her offer.[5]

The first part of her speech concerns roads of inquiry, ὁδοὶ διζήσιος.[6] Fragments B2, B6, B7, and B8.1–49 clearly belong to this part of the speech; and it is usually thought that B3, B4, and B5 belong here too. In B2, B6, and B7 the goddess enjoins the young man not to follow certain roads, explaining why they would not be viable. In B8.1–49 the goddess characterizes the road she recommends, and argues for its merits.

At B8.50, the goddess announces that she will change the subject and discuss the opinions of mortals, the second thing that she had promised at B1.29–30. B9 appears to continue the discussion, begun at 8.53, of mortals' account of the world as Light and Night. B10 through B18, which concern cosmology, astronomy, physiology, psychology, and the origin of gods, are also generally thought to belong to the section on the opinions of mortals. Simplicius, our source for B19, asserts that it appeared following a section on the ordering of the sensible things (τῶν αἰσθητῶν διακόσμησιν).[7] This suggests that B19 follows

---

4   Sextus Empiricus, *Adversus mathematicos* vii, 111–114, in Coxon 2009, 183.

5   While she does not in the extant fragments claim that anything she says details the ἀλήθεια, she does say at B8.50–51 that what she has said so far was ἀμφὶς ἀληθείης, around or concerning ἀλήθεια. This suggests that whatever in the goddess's speech preceded B.50 was supposed to be at least part of the locus of the young man's learning the heart of ἀλήθεια.

6   B2.2, B6.3, B7.2, and by implication B2.4, B2.6, B6.9, B7.3, B8.1, B8.18.

7   Simplicius, *in Aristotelis de Caelo Commentarii* 558, in Coxon 2009, 233. No form of αἰσθητός occurs in Parmenides, but διακόσμησις recalls διάκοσμον at Parmenides B8.60.

the remarks on the opinions of mortals (B8.53–61, B9–B18), as these remarks address observable things.

Let us note three things about this structure:

a. All of the arguments regarding ἐόν, what-is or being; and with the *possible* exception of B4, all discussion of ἐόν; appear within the goddess's account of roads of inquiry. I will argue that Parmenides was exploring the requisites of inquiry in these passages.

b. The proem, which presents a context for the goddess's speech, is couched in the opinions of some mortals, viz., Greeks of Parmenides' time: people who believed in humans, horses, divinities, chariots, motion, Night, Day, and so on. The second part of the goddess's speech is an account of what she says are the opinions of mortals (as at B1.30), or mortal opinions (B8.51). On the surface, it may not seem that any mortals have ever held those opinions. However, I will propose a way in which the opinions the goddess attributes to mortals fit with the opinions on which the proem relies. If this is correct, then the tale of the journey shows us Parmenides' conceptual starting-points.

c. The part of the goddess's speech that concerns roads of inquiry is thus framed by the opinions of mortals.[8] Given the goddess's description of the opinions of mortals, I will argue, the portion of the speech about ἐόν and roads of inquiry is also not only framed in but derived from the opinions of mortals.

II   Roads of Inquiry and (Apparent) Requisites of Inquiry

As noted above, the goddess's arguments concerning the characteristics of what-is appear within her discussion of roads of inquiry, and the most sustained surviving arguments appear in her discussion of the road of inquiry that she recommends (B8.1–49).

What, then, is a road of inquiry, ὁδὸς διζήσιος? We may understand it as a series of oriented steps that one takes in inquiring or seeking. As the goddess says at B2.2, 6.1–2, 7.2, 8.7–9, 8.17, and probably 8.34–36, being on a road of inquiry involves speaking of (identifying; λέγειν, φάσθαι) and conceiving of or recognizing (νοεῖν) what-is. The goddess says that the road she discusses at B8.1–49 is more conducive to inquiry than the alternatives. Following a path

---

8 Cf. Miller 2006, 15–16.

that is (more) conducive to inquiry requires that one say and conceive of or recognize things in a different way than following other paths.

Parmenides' goddess's account of the road she recommends for inquiry oriented by ἀλήθεια seems to require the following:

- recognition of some sort of principle of non-contradiction;
- recognition and articulation of distinctions, division, and motion or change;
- recognition of some sort of order and regularity in what we say is (associated with δίκη, B8.14);
- conceiving of what-is in such a way that nothing lacks implications or causes (associated with ἀνάγκη, B8.30);
- conceiving of what-is in such a way that the whole of what-is and its relationships is continuous (associated with μοῖρα, B8.37).

Let us now consider why inquiry might seem to require these features, and where and how Parmenides' goddess indicates that it does.

First of all, then, a road of inquiry admits of a direction and distinct identifiable steps. Next, in order to be able to pose and to answer questions, one must have some non-contradictory way of identifying both what one seeks, and that which is not that which one seeks. For example, to inquire after or seek salamanders, one needs to be able to identify which things are salamanders, which things are not salamanders, and how to tell one salamander and perhaps one kind of salamander from another (if one intends to count the salamanders). One also needs to be able to identify what steps to take in order to seek salamanders. Walking around aimlessly is not seeking salamanders; looking only on top of snow and ice or in the sky is not, under normal circumstances, seeking or inquiring about salamanders; for certain species of salamanders, ruling out looking under rocks and logs or in water is not seeking salamanders. Identifying likely habitats and looking in them in ways that do not drive off or destroy salamanders, then eliminating choices once tried, would be a way to seek salamanders.

All of these features involve difference, involve being able to distinguish and identify what one considers to be things; and also involve acknowledging some sort of change or motion. As we will see shortly, this is just the kind of world for which the Light and Night of the goddess's account of mortals' opinions provides support.

But more is required of a road where inquiry is to be viable, and the goddess tells us about that too. The other requisites for inquiry turn out to be very much at odds with the ones I have noted so far. Yet they also support them, and (as we will see) are derived from those same mortal opinions that fostered them.

What are these other requisites of inquiry? They are very much what the goddess says in B8 that δίκη, ἀνάγκη, and μοῖρα enforce.[9]

I have noted that seeking salamanders requires us to identify which things are salamanders and which are not. We cannot seek a thing if we have no stable criteria for recognizing it, or if we cannot know any valid principles that govern its relationships through all of its changes. Thus we must claim and recognize some order and regularity in what we say is, if we are to be able to inquire. In order to be able to ask questions or to direct our seeking, we must hold that the general characteristics that we invoke when we identify things always bear the same relationships to one another. Greek terminology for this is δίκη. Δίκη connotes the idea of an order or standard, of a consistent way things are, and of a way that is appropriate. It is associated with the enforcing or effecting of order, balance, right, regularities, justice, and that which is appropriate.

We can follow clues and use the process of elimination just when we conceive that there is a stable underlying order of things, and that each thing has stable identifiable proper characteristics, or that it changes in consistent ways—when we speak and conceive of the world, in effect, as subject to δίκη. Then we must suppose that the characteristics that we identify for use in our inquiries must not in a random way come to be, change, or perish. If they did, the terms that we use in order to inquire—indeed, the very use of terms—would be meaningless. Those general characteristics, those standards, must stand in certain stable relations to one another if inquiry is to be possible.

Then to be able to use a process of elimination, we evidently must conceive that there is conservation of what-is. We must conceive, that is, that no thing can come from or perish into nothing, and that relevant processes of change are regular and traceable. We cannot hold that either the whole of what is or any particular thing came to be out of anything or out of nothing, if we are to be able to seek anything. If we were to hold that anything came to be from something other than what is, we could not with consistency also claim to have terms with stable meanings with which to identify anything. Inquiry would not be possible. Similarly, if inquiry is to be possible, we cannot hold that what is

---

9 On δίκη, ἀνάγκη, and μοῖρα in Parmenides, see Fränkel 1960, 162–173; Mansfeld 1964, especially 261–273; Vlastos 1993; Mourelatos 2008, 25–29, 148–154, and 160–162; Austin 1986 Chapter Four; Collobert 1993, 50–59; Schürmann 1996, 114–120; Robbiano 2006 Chapter Six; Cherubin 2001, 296–301, and 2009. On senses and associations of δίκη, ἀνάγκη, and μοῖρα in Greek literature in and before Parmenides' time, see Hirzel 1966/1907, especially 108–125, 389–402, 426ff.; Onians 1951 Part III, especially 327–338; Fränkel 1960, 163–164; Schreckenberg 1964; Lloyd-Jones 1971; Detienne 1990, 33–34, 60–61, 112–113, 131–138; Cherubin 2001, 297–298n24; Robbiano 2006, 155–160.

can generate itself or something other than itself. We also cannot hold that what is can perish utterly, that is, that a thing or a characteristic can become nothing. If what is could perish, there would be no grounds for claiming that there were any regularities, for all patterns would disappear. No meanings or distinctions would be stable. Inquiry would not be possible. These are exactly the conditions that δίκη enforces in shackling ἐόν at 8.12–14.

But then the very requirements we had for identifying particular things through ephemeral steps in time are incompatible with any change or motion. In other words, some of what inquiry appears to require, that which was associated with δίκη, is at odds with other things inquiry appears to require, such as passage of time.

This kind of conflict arises not only for what δίκη enforces on what-is, but also for what ἀνάγκη and μοῖρα enforce. It is a systematic feature of the goddess's account of how what-is is on the road of inquiry she recommends. Here is a brief summary of how this kind of conflict arises with regard to what ἀνάγκη and μοῖρα enforce.

The process of elimination, or any deductive inference (such as the goddess herself uses), requires that one conceive of what-is such that there is nothing that lacks implications, and no missing links in causal or deductive chains. Parmenides alludes to this at B8.30 by saying that ἀνάγκη binds what-is so that it is appropriate for it not to be incomplete. These features derive from the traditional associations of ἀνάγκη. Ἀνάγκη was associated with necessity, including the fact that certain consequences follow necessarily from certain conditions. Ἀνάγκη is then a requisite for inquiry and inference. If ἀνάγκη is not in effect, anything (or nothing) could follow from anything. We could not look for anything.

But consider causes and effects, and binding. These involve, they are defined on, change, difference, and motion. The goddess says that ἀνάγκη is associated with what-is being "not incomplete" and not lacking. "Following" implies that something was not complete, or perhaps lacked something; and that some motion or change occurs. Yet (and, therefore) the goddess says that ἀνάγκη binds what is to remain the same and in the same way (B8.29).

According to Parmenides' goddess, μοῖρα binds what-is to be whole, unmoving, and unaccompanied (B8.36–38). Μοῖρα, usually translated as 'fate' or 'portion,' was traditionally understood to assure that each thing and person had a proper place and certain characteristics proper to it: a proper or due share of what is. Clearly (based on what we take to be), this must be in place if inquiry is to be possible. We could not tell what to look for or what we were looking at if each thing did not have characteristics proper to it and a certain place or set of relationships with respect to others.

We can see how μοῖρα would bind τὸ ἐόν in the way Parmenides' goddess mentions. While 'οὖλον' sometimes means 'complete,' which sense was associated with ἀνάγκη (B8.32–33), 'οὖλον' can also mean 'without internal divisions,' 'all of a piece,' 'not composed of discrete parts.' Indeed the goddess had mentioned that on this road what-is is continuous (B8.6 and 8.22); this appears to be an argument for that. If the whole of things and their relations was not continuous, if it had gaps, then causal and explanatory linkages could not be ascertained, and we could not identify a proper place or range, a proper μοῖρα, for each thing. Then we could not identify things with any assurance, and could not even begin to inquire. Similarly, if the complex of things and relations were unstable (not ἀκίνητον, 8.38), we could not determine what was proper to each. If something else, something discontinuous with τὸ ἐόν, were to be alongside of it (ἄλλο πάρεξ τοῦ ἐόντος, 8.37), then we could not account for anything that is without accounting for that which is outside of τὸ ἐόν. But outside of τὸ ἐόν could not be what-is-not, according to Parmenides' goddess.[10]

Again, conflicts arise. According to the goddess, μοῖρα binds what-is to be whole and unmoving. But μοῖρα is supposed to have to do with fate (involving change and thus movement), and to do with shares or parts. Was not μοῖρα defined on things with places and roles relative to other things? Things that undergo processes with specific proper outcomes? Division into shares? A share is defined as not being the whole; lack of movement would seem to rule out fate playing out in time.

What all of this shows is that the requisites of inquiry that the goddess identifies are at odds with each other. That is a problem given that one of those requisites was non-contradiction.[11] But we cannot simply go forward in inquiry by selecting some consistent subset of requisites of inquiry, by adopting some conception of what-is that does not harbor internal conflicts; for the requisites of inquiry are interdependent. In other words, we cannot simply opt to say that what-is is one, and reject multiplicity, as for example Melissus would have us do. I think Parmenides recognized this. More specifically, I suggest that he recognized that the argument for the inadequacy of mortals' opinions was couched in and derived from mortals' opinions. Let us turn to that now.

---

10   Not only do these features support inquiry, but they also must be in place if we are to be able to give the ἀλήθεια. See Cherubin 2009.

11   Clark 2008 has shown how non-contradiction and excluded middle would be incompatible with the premise that things can differ or change, and has identified Parmenides as suggesting this (26ff.). Clark does not address the question of what inquiry appears to require, but argues that "the laws [of logic] cannot be read off from experience, nor are they formal conditions for reasonable speech" (25–26).

PARMENIDES, LIARS, AND MORTAL INCOMPLETENESS 9

III Our Starting-Points: The Opinions of Mortals

The goddess mentions that mortals claim that what-is comes to be, that it perishes, that it changes place and color (B8.39–41), that it in some way is not (B7.1), and even that what-is and what-is not are the same and not the same (B6.8–9). She goes on to detail what she says are fundamental aspects of mortals' opinions in B8.53–61 and B9. Scholars have long noted that what the goddess presents as the opinions of mortals was not articulated in so many words by anyone before Parmenides. It does not reproduce known statements by any group or individual who would have been familiar to Parmenides.[12] That no one had previously stated that what-is comprises only what the goddess calls Light and Night does not imply that no one had such a conception. One might not express, or even necessarily take note of, an implicit supposition or conceptual framework. This may be so especially for a supposition or conception that is a foundational component of more commonly expressed aspects of one's worldview.[13]

I suggest that there is a way in which what the goddess says in those passages about Light and Night really does fit with mortals' (our) opinions; and that the proem and the goddess's arguments about the road she recommends—the one that conflicts with mortals' opinions—are couched in and derived from those same opinions of mortals.[14]

In fragment B8, lines 51–61, and B9, the goddess claims that mortals lay down two γνώμας to specify μορφάς—we lay down two judgments or opinions to specify forms. These are Light (φάος) and Night (νύξ). Each is all that the other is not. Light is lightweight, mild, fiery, and tends upward. Night is heavy, dense, dark, and generally opposite to Light.

Together they afford distinction, division, and change.

A. *Distinction and Division.* Light and Night as described by the goddess enable the use of negation in describing what-is. They not only make possible but obey a principle of non-contradiction. They also involve a principle of excluded middle (B9.4 says either that nothing has a share in neither Light nor Night, or that neither Light nor Night has a share in nothing). What it is to be Light is

---

12 See Long 1975, 90; Benardete 1998, 197; Curd 2004, 116–123; Cherubin 2005, 3–4n9.

13 Cf. Aristotle, *Metaphysics* 981b27ff.: "... τὴν ὀνομαζομένην σοφίαν περὶ τὰ πρῶτα αἴτια καὶ τὰς ἀρχὰς ὑπολαμβάνουσι πάντες" (all people suppose that what is called 'wisdom' is concerned with the first causes and principles). Aristotle does not identify anyone who has said this outright; rather, he infers that people suppose this, based on an examination of other things he reports are commonly said.

14 The view that the proem is couched in and relies on conceptions matching what the goddess presents in B8.51–61 and B9 is not new; see for example Miller 1979, 16 and 20–21.

precisely what it is not to be Night, and vice versa. Things may contain both, but evidently not in the same way in the same place at the same time.

B. *Change*. In so far as Light is fiery and aetherial, it seems to move upward, to illuminate, and to heat. Night seems to move downward, to cool, to block, to darken and perhaps dampen (in both senses of the word). As Light is "mild" (ἤπιον, B8.57), it would seem to be yielding, to allow things to move through it, to offer little or no resistance; whereas Night would confer solidity and the ability to move through the areas of less resistance.

Together Light and Night would seem also to enable sensation to happen. Light and Night certainly invoke space. In addition, we need, or seem to need, both light and darkness to see; we do not see in either unbroken light or unbroken dark (note the use of ἀΐδηλα to describe the sun in B10.3 and the related ἀδαῆ to describe Night in 8.59).[15] We seem to need both cold and hot to feel either one; we seem to need both solidity and unresistance to feel any object *as* an object; Greeks had the idea as early as Homer that we need both solidity and airiness or hollowness to hear.[16] It is not hard to see how Light and Night could also account for our ability to perceive smells (as results of heating, as carried on moving air) and textures (as affected by heating, cooling, changes in density).

Fragments B10, 11, 12, 14, 15, probably B16 and B18, and a number of the testimonia indicate that Parmenides used Light and Night to try to account for familiar phenomena such as the gestation of animals of different sexes, the movements and natures of the heavenly bodies, and the work of at least some of the gods.

This is one way in which what the goddess says of the "opinions of mortals" fits the opening tale of the journey. The journey involves movement through space, various sensations, different sexes, humans, other animals, gods, a variety of sights and sounds, and of course Night and Day. But there is another way in which the account of the opinions of mortals suggests the underlying assumptions of the tale of the journey: it fosters claims about being and not-being, division and distinction, multiplicity and unity, identity and difference, and non-contradiction. It is this second cohort of suppositions that is central to the goddess's account of the road of inquiry on which what-is is, and that is challenged by her account of that road.

---

15   Cf. Mourelatos 2013, 96ff.

16   *Odyssey* 12.173–177.

IV   The Goddess's Account of ἐόν and the Requisites of Inquiry

Commentators have of course noted that the goddess uses plurals, negations (references to not-being), and references to motions or actions in her speech to the young man of the chariot. It certainly makes sense for her to phrase the introduction to her lesson in terms the young man, and Parmenides' readers, will find familiar. But when she reaches the discussion of the road of inquiry she recommends—the one on which signs indicate that ἐόν is ungenerated, unperishing, whole of one kind, unmoving, complete, not admitting of "was" or "will be," one, and continuous (B8.1–6)—in that description too, and in the arguments for it, she uses those negations, plurals, and references to motions and changes.

A. *Avoidable Uses Designed to Produce Maximum Conflict.* In fact, Parmenides has her use negations, plurals, and references to motions and changes even more often, and in ways that generate more conflicts than she might need to. He has her use these in ways he has shown that he knows how to avoid. This is a strong hint that Parmenides was aware both of the extent to which the goddess's arguments start from mortals' opinions or something functionally equivalent, and of the conflicts that these opinions engender for inquiry.

Examples include γένεσις ... ἀπέσβεσται ("coming-to-be has been extinguished") at B8.21; γένεσις καὶ ὄλεθρος / τῆλε μάλ᾽ ἐπλάγχθησαν, ἀπῶσε δὲ πίστις ἀληθής ("coming-to-be and perishing wandered very far off, and true assurance pushed them away") at 8.27–28; and arguably πάντοθεν εὐκύκλου σφαίρης ἐναλίγκιον ὄγκῳ ("from all sides like the bulk of a well-rounded ball") at 8.43. That is, although she has said that on the road of inquiry she recommends there is no "was" or "will be" (8.5), the goddess uses past tenses, or tenses that refer to completed processes ('ἀπέσβεσται,' 'ἐπλάγχθησαν,' 'ἀπῶσε'). Although she has said that what-is does not move (8.4, 8.26), 8.27–28 refers to 'wandering' and 'pushing away.' Although she has said that what-is does not come-to-be or perish (8.3), 'extinguishing' certainly sounds like perishing, and 'wandering' and 'pushing' sound like coming-to-be different. Although she has said that what-is is all alike, with no internal or external divisions or differences (8.5, 8.22), being "like the bulk of a sphere" would seem to imply some sort of difference: a sphere is not the only shape; and a sphere has a top and a bottom, a surface and a middle, left and right sides, and so on.

Moreover, would something not need to be in order to wander, to be extinguished, or to be pushed away? But the goddess has said that on this road what-is does not come-to-be or perish, that coming-to-be and perishing are not (8.3, 8.5, 8.13–14, 8.21; compare 8.29). And if being extinguished is a kind of change or coming-to-be, is the goddess then saying that coming-to-be both is and is not—the very kind of contradictory statement she warns her pupil against (8.15–18; 8.46–48, B6.4–9, B7.1)?

Parmenides indicates that he knows how to have the goddess discuss how ἐόν is to be spoken of and conceived on the recommended road, without having to refer to past or future, to sensible things or things with divisions or parts, or to the being of what is-not. For example, at B8.6–10 she argues that her listener would not be able to seek a birth or source for ἐόν and that he could not speak or conceive of it as it is not (or that he could not speak or conceive of what-is in the manner of what is not). At 8.13–15 she says that Δίκη does not allow coming-to-be or perishing. At 8.16–18, she warns that in accordance with ἀνάγκη a road on which what-is is not is ἀνόητον ἀνώνυμον, not conceived or named (inconceivable and unnameable).

Certainly the goddess needs to make some use of plurals, negations, and references to differences and to processes in time in order to communicate with her mortal pupil; and Parmenides needs to use these in order to communicate with us. We have seen (sections II and III) that this causes problems. But the goddess's references to extinguishing, pushing, wandering, and passage of time; her apparent acknowledgment of the presence of what is-not; and her use of the ball or sphere analogy are unnecessary. The presence in the fragments of the unnecessary and obviously problematic formulations of this kind suggests that Parmenides wants to draw our attention to the depth and breadth of our enmeshment in mortal opinions, and to the extent to which her own arguments are expressed through and rely on those opinions.

B. *Dependence on Mortals' Opinions or the Equivalent.* Let us note further that the account of ἐόν on the road of inquiry that the goddess recommends is not only expressed in the terms of, but depends on, the opinions of mortals or suppositions functionally equivalent to them. Recall that the arguments concerning what-is occur within the context of the goddess's discussion of roads of inquiry. That is, the goddess announces at the end of B1 that her listener is to learn the heart of ἀλήθεια and the opinions of mortals. But then in B2, the fragment that seems to come next earliest in her speech, she opens a discussion of "just which are the only roads of inquiry to conceive."[17] After identifying at least one such road as impracticable (incoherent and/or contradictory) in B6 and B7, the goddess discusses the "remaining" road in B8.1–49. This appears to be the road that the goddess had recommended as associated with Πειθώ (persuasion) and Ἀληθείη at B2.3–4. It is in B6, B7, and B8.1–49, in discussions of

---

17   αἵπερ ὁδοὶ μοῦναι διζήσιός εἰσι νοῆσαι, B2.2.

that road, that Parmenides' goddess character presents arguments concerning how what-is is.

These arguments are based in mortals' opinions. By this I mean first of all that their premises, axioms, and principles of inference come from things specific actual mortals believed: for example, the people around Parmenides would have believed that δίκη, ἀνάγκη, μοῖρα, and θέμις operated in the universe; that νόημα, divinities, humans, roads, and bonds existed; and that some sort of principle of non-contradiction held. A second way that the arguments are based in mortals' opinions is that they are founded on what the Light-Night scheme provides: a conceptual framework that underpins negation, distinction, multiplicity, difference, motion, and change (including some sort of coming to be and perishing). Thus a different framework of complementary opposites that would work to underpin the same things and that would equally provide for sensation, in other words something functionally equivalent to the Light-Night scheme, would work just as well.

V   Implications: Liar-type Paradoxes

What does this mean for the import of Parmenides' fragments taken together? The goddess, feature of the universe of mortals' opinions, has used mortals' opinions to show that mortals' opinions are flawed. What is going on here is more than a *reductio ad absurdum*. In this case, the terms in which the argument was conducted, the terms through which the implications were drawn, the terms through which we express the conclusion, are what have been reduced to absurdity. For the goddess's argument was about what it would take in order to be able to infer at all. We have arrived at a sort of liar paradox.

I have called it "*a sort of* liar paradox" rather than "*the* liar paradox" because it is constituted somewhat differently from well-known exemplars of this sort of paradox. The most familiar exemplars are statements such as "This statement is false" and "All Cretans constantly lie" [uttered by a Cretan]. As Yale Weiss astutely notes in his comments, liar paradoxes as currently understood generally have to do with truth-values. The kind of thing I suggest appears in Parmenides has a different form, and does not turn entirely on truth-values. It is something like "Mortals' opinions imply that mortals' opinions are flawed," or "If mortals' opinions are true then mortals' opinions are flawed and so possibly not true," spoken by a mortal; or "As a mortal I find that if the opinions I use to inquire are true, then they cannot be true." Or again, "From the suppositions that make inquiry and inference possible, given my opinions as a mortal, it follows— I infer—that mortals' opinions undermine inference."

One source of this difference between what Parmenides generates and familiar liar paradoxes is the fact that Parmenides' goddess recommends a road of inquiry that she associates with ἀλήθεια, and ἀλήθεια is not exactly the same as truth. In Greek writers to Parmenides' time, ἀλήθεια was opposed not only to falsity or falsehood, but also to oblivion, obscurity, unclarity, unreality, incompleteness of an account, lack of awareness, and hiddenness.[18] To give a false report would not be to give the ἀλήθεια. But neither would an account give the ἀλήθεια if it was true but overlooked, omitted, concealed, or left obscure some important feature; or included distortions, confusions, unclarities, indeterminacies, or features that undermine the speaker's reliability along with accurate portions.

Someone might object at this point by saying that Parmenides provides us with ways to avoid falling into these kinds of paradoxes. A δαίμων such as Parmenides' goddess would be supposed by mortals to be self-sufficient, and to have understanding beyond what a human could have. Thus Parmenides' goddess does not need to inquire. When she utters her arguments, it might be objected, she is not caught in something like a liar paradox. My response is that she *is* a sort of liar paradox. She is a figure from, an artefact of, mortals' opinions. She is what mortals think an immortal would be. She is in many senses what mortals think we are not. She is part of the same ecology of mortals' opinions that generated the paradox. So she "is" a kind of liar or liar-like paradox in the sense that she is supposed to have a grasp of what what-is is really like. If it is as she says, then she does not exist as she is described. And the way she says it is, again, is an inference from the very opinions she shows to be flawed. In other words, Parmenides' use of the goddess character does not enable him to avoid liar-like paradoxes. It ramifies the paradoxes.

VI   Where Does This Leave Us?

What does this imply about the account of the recommended road of inquiry, and what does it imply about the opinions of mortals? I propose that it implies that the two are interdependent, even symbiotic, though not symmetrical. The opinions of mortals, or the suppositions involved in them, need the suppositions of the favored road in order to support communication, predictive success, and inquiry (and to support the inference to the conflicting requisites of inquiry the road represents). This is so both for opinions that mortals are

---

18   See Cole 1983, Detienne 1990 (especially Chapters 1–2), Germani 1988 (especially 178–185), and Krischer 1965.

known to have held, and for the Light-Night conception that the goddess presents, as this provides a framework that supports key features of familiar mortal opinions. The requisites of inquiry on the road need the opinions of mortals in the sense that they are derived from those opinions, defined on them; and also in the sense that inquiry is not possible without difference, passage of time, etc. Thus we cannot simply choose to accept one side rather than the other (mortals' opinions or the characterization of what-is on the road the goddess recommends). They are interdependent; when we choose one we have chosen the other. And to choose neither? How would that be possible, when choosing, as Wians 2006 has so well illustrated, requires accepting non-contradiction? Non-contradiction in turn depends on accepting that there are distinct things such that in at least some cases, to be one is not to be another; and thus on accepting mortals' opinions.

How if at all would a Parmenides who says this kind of thing be contributing to inquiry, and to what would become philosophy? Some very tentative suggestions as to what Parmenides has offered us and what kind of contribution it makes:

(a) Speaking of non-contradiction, Parmenides has identified that kind of principle as fundamental to inquiry, and has explored some of its implications and limitations. He has also identified some other things that seem (from our standpoint in mortals' opinions) to be requisites for inquiry.

In so doing, he has shown one way in which mortals' opinions "work," up to a point anyway. That is, mortals' opinions appear to allow us to communicate, to infer deductively, to ask questions, to seek or inquire. It is through them that we arrive at the conclusion that they are flawed and incomplete, that they fall short of what mortals conceive as ἀλήθεια even when they are "true." The meanings of mortals' claims depend on contradictions. By making this manifest, Parmenides has enabled us to learn quite a lot. Not least, this demonstration of incompleteness, of failure to fulfill what ἀλήθεια requires, is a constant reminder of what it is to be mortal. Here is what I mean:

Why does the goddess always call the opinions that rest on the Light-Night framework "mortal opinions," or "mortals' opinions"?[19] Why not refer to these at least some of the time as "human opinions"? What is the relationship between relying on, conceiving in terms of, these opinions; and being mortal?

Here is a suggestion. In one temporal way, to be mortal is to be limited and to be immortal is to be unlimited. Our human lives have beginnings and ends in time, whereas the Greek gods were understood as undying (ἀθάνατος,

---

19   B1.30 and 8.51; 8.53 and 8.39 (what mortals lay down); unknowing humans are also called 'mortals' (rather than 'humans') at B6.4.

ἄμβροτος), living without end.[20] But there is another sense in which mortality reflects incompleteness and lack of fulfillment, in contrast to divine completeness and fulfillment; and the opinions of Parmenides' mortals manifest this.

Pre-Parmenidean poetry is full of references to gods as "fulfillers" of desires, oaths, plans. The gods have the awareness and capability to fulfill their own desires, oaths, and plans; and also frequently need to assist, or at least be willing to allow, the fulfillment of humans' aims. Humans frequently lack the knowledge and/or the capability to realize their own plans (*Odyssey* 1.249; on the difficulties in figuring out how to accomplish goals, *Iliad* 9.625). Gods are supposed to be self-sufficient; we are not. Our existence and our flourishing depend on things beyond our control.

I would like to suggest that Parmenides' fragments imply that the opinions of mortals reflect to us a parallel result on our understanding. The fragments make us aware of our lack at a fundamental level. (In one sense, to be mortal is to be aware that one is lacking.) Mortals' opinions, Parmenides shows, are incommensurable with what those very same opinions imply that inquiry and ἀλήθεια require. This is not saying that mortals' opinions fall short of what ἀλήθεια would require, and that conceiving of a unitary and unmoving ἐόν (if that were even possible) would fulfill what ἀλήθεια requires. For the goddess's account of how we are to speak and conceive of what-is on the recommended road of inquiry was itself framed in and derived from mortals' opinions. The goddess is a goddess, and immortal, *modulo* mortals' opinions. The incommensurability, and hence the incompleteness of our journeys of inquiry, are a function of this internal conflict, this incompatibility within mortals' opinions. Our lack is ἀπείρων, unended, indefinite. That is not entirely a bad thing, if meaning

---

20   Hesiod's account at *Theogony* 116ff. is usually understood to mean that all of the gods came to be, and thus that their lifetimes were unlimited in only one direction. Some scholars, such as Gantz 1996 (3), argue that 'γένετ'' in 116 could be meant in the sense of 'was,' so that Chaos was unborn; but see Miller 2001 (10) for arguments against this. There are other candidates for an unborn source of some gods. Oceanus, possibly with Tethys, is called 'θεῶν γένεσιν' at *Iliad* 14.201 and 302; no birth is mentioned for these two. Miller 2001 (9–12) argues that Hesiod implies that Tartarus is in some sense an unborn source of all other gods, that Tartarus was before becoming differentiated from Earth. Also, by Parmenides' time, Musaeus B14 and Epimenides B5 had proposed primordial gods that may not have come to be, and Pherecydes (B1/Diogenes Laertius i.119) had proposed that some god or gods were unborn as well as undying. Xenophanes B14 suggested that the belief that gods came to be is inaccurate and likely impious. These were more consistent with the notion of a god as self-sufficient and able to complete or fulfill aims, and thus threw human limitations into sharper relief.

depends on contradiction; for we, unlike immortals, will have reason to seek and to think that we can gain thereby.

The fragments do not suggest or imply that mortals *must* hold the opinions the goddess attributes to us, that we are somehow compelled to have this or some functionally equivalent conceptual framework.[21] Indeed, to suggest something like that would be to suggest that we can state, though our current conceptions, what the truth of our situation is; and that would be self-contradictory. It would also be to suggest that we can know what it takes to have a correct conception of what-is, and that we can know that we can have such a conception. But this would be to suggest that we know that what is is as we say (or can say) it is, and that the requisites of inquiry hold; and this is assuming the desired conclusion. It is incompatible with what Parmenides' fragments say. It is also hubristic and unjust, ἄδικος: it relies on the manifestly unwarranted and inaccurate assumption that what we say is (what we want or are accustomed or are pressured to say is) is what is. It relies on the assumption that the way we have learned to conceive of what-is provides an adequate and accurate account of what-is, that it neither omits nor distorts.

Then if we may not have to hold the particular set of opinions we hold, what can we do to learn better, now that we can see what their flaws seem to be? We can investigate the consequences of our starting assumptions, and then investigate the consequences of the assumptions we used in that investigation; this too would be an indefinite series, but it would mean a gradual shedding of some of our more flawed ideas. But more than that, we can pay attention to what Parmenides' goddess identified (*modulo* mortals' opinions) as the requisites of inquiry. For these are what appear to stand in the way of our witting or unwitting embrace of injustice, imbalance, and overstepping.[22]

---

21 Tor 2015 has suggested that humans must conceive of or apprehend what-is in terms of the opposites that are incorporated in Light and Night (8, 18ff.). But the fragments neither state nor imply such a necessity, and B8.53 and 55 seem to challenge that idea: to "lay down" such oppositions is not at all to receive them "ineluctably" or "passively" (8).

22 In this way one might see in Parmenides an anticipation not only of a central question of Plato's *Meno* and *Phaedo*, namely how to seek and examine something when one lacks knowledge of what and how it is (*Meno* 80d, cf.71b; *Phaedo* 96c-97c); but also of the response to the question in those dialogues (*Meno* 85c-e, 97e-98b; *Phaedo* 100a ff.), minus the references to anamnesis. Regarding the possibility of mortal limits to clarity, cf. *Meno* 85c-d, "will understand as precisely as anyone." On the possibility that the investigation might proceed indefinitely, cf. *Phaedo* 101d-e (it is not clear that one necessarily will reach a final adequate hypothesis) and 107b-c. I am grateful to William Wians for emphasizing the importance of these prefigurings of Plato.

(b) One can see in this a connection to B1.31–32, where the goddess announces that the young man of the chariot is to learn the opinions of mortals, "how the things that seem (τὰ δοκοῦντα)/ Need to be accepted to be altogether [going] throughout all things."

We have seen that the goddess's account of the opinions of mortals—the Light-Night conceptual scheme—actually does say something informative about the underlying suppositions of what mortals believe. And we have seen that this is useful in communicating things that could be true, or that depend on meanings that appear to be shared and appear for a while to be stable. Mortals' opinions allow us to seek explanations, and to find something that appears to work like explanation, thanks to the assumption of δίκη, ἀνάγκη, and μοῖρα. That is conducive to what we would call scientific investigation, or more conducive than alternatives such as non-causal reasoning, or such as might-makes-right models of meaning.

As Sisko and Weiss 2015 (43–44) have noted, in B10 Parmenides' goddess explicitly offers to help her pupil gain *knowledge* of the workings of the heavens. Recent scholarship has brought out more and more of Parmenides' success at accounting for some aspects of the observable world.[23] Parmenides made the discoveries that the Morning Star and the Evening Star were the same object and that the moon shines by light "borrowed" from the sun. Beyond this, as Rossetti 2016, Graham 2013, Popper 1998, and others have recently argued, Parmenides realized that the moon and the earth were spherical. His discoveries are explanations that have a certain kind of predictive success, or at very least descriptive and explanatory success.[24]

That is, there are not grounds to say that Parmenides' Light-Night framework, or any of his discoveries in astronomy or physiology, are by themselves sufficient to enable us to make precise quantitative predictions about the behavior of anything. Nor do we have reason to say that Parmenides' discoveries involved or enabled the prediction of experimental results. In those modern senses of 'predictive success,' it would be inappropriate to say that Parmenides' discoveries as detailed in B10–B12 and B14–B19 enable predictive success.

---

23   Bollack 2006; Graham 2006; Cerri 2008; Wacziarg 2008; Mourelatos 2013.

24   I am grateful to Yale Weiss for pressing the question of whether or to what extent Parmenides' efforts in the discussion of the opinions of mortals are oriented toward what would today be called 'predictive success.' As Germani and Krischer have argued, 'ἔτυμος' could mean something close to 'accurate in prediction' when used of dreams and prophecies, whereas 'ἀληθής' was not used with that sense. It would be possible for Parmenides to suggest that mortals' opinions were valuable for practical description and fairly accurate qualitative predictions of certain natural phenomena (such as the appearance of the moon or of Venus) without saying that these descriptions or predictions gave ἀλήθεια.

However, they can be seen to enable successful predictions in a broader sense that is more appropriate to the period. First, B10–B12, B14, and B15 all invoke either Light (via fire), Night, or both. Testimonia suggest that B16–B18 also invoked Light and Night.[25] This implies that Parmenides tried to show how the Light-Night framework could account for the cosmos, its contents, and their workings: a kind of descriptive and explanatory success, given the observations and knowledge available. Second, Parmenides' proposals about the shapes of the earth and the moon, about the source of the moon's light,[26] and about the identity of the Morning Star and the Evening Star would help people predict where in the sky the Evening Star would rise and set, how an eclipse would progress (for example, what the moon might look like at a given stage of a lunar eclipse, how its appearance might change), and perhaps when some eclipses would occur.[27] As for whether predictive success was either a goal for Parmenides or a desideratum in the development of his work in astronomy, Graham 2013 (99–100, 174) argues that the proposal about the moon shining by reflecting the sun's light predicts the observed shape of the illuminated portion of the moon at each location in its observed path through the sky over the period of a lunar month. Certainly Greeks of Parmenides' time were familiar with both the path and the sequence of variations in the moon's shape.

This is not to say that Parmenides' discoveries are *deductions* from the axioms that what-is is Light and Night. Rather, I suggest that Parmenides' goddess's assertions about celestial phenomena are illustrations of how we can account for observable phenomena in a way that affords descriptive, explanatory, and (loosely) predictive success by using the Light-Night scheme and the tools it affords (non-contradiction, excluded middle, conservation/δίκη, etc.). I would conjecture that the remarks about physiology are also illustrations, if less successful illustrations from our point of view today.[28]

---

25   See for example Theophrastus *De sensibus* 1.1–4, in Stratton 1917/1967; Merlan 1976; Henn 2003 (especially 136); Bollack 2006; Journée 2012.

26   See Rossetti 2016, 619ff. On evidence for Anaxagoras's and other later uses of Parmenides' insights for prediction of the look and behavior of celestial bodies, see Graham 2013.

27   By the same token, B17 might have offered what was thought to be support for predictions of the sex of a baby before it was born, on the basis of its mother's abdominal sensations during pregnancy.

28   Cf. Popper 1998, 122–123.

VII   Concluding

On the road of inquiry that Parmenides' goddess recommends, one is to say and conceive that what-is is one, unmoving, continuous, ungenerated, undestroyed, complete, and undivided. Yet in order to make the case for this road, the goddess uses negations, distinctions, divisions, and references to generation and destruction. The requisites of inquiry that she outlines are at odds with other features that inquiry appears to require, such as defining one's object and taking a series of steps. At the same time, the requisites she outlines are defined on, and follow from, a belief in a world of multiple things, some of which move or come to be or perish.

The goddess herself, *qua* goddess, is an artefact of the worldview that she criticizes. Therefore, I have argued, the goddess's arguments manifest something like a liar paradox: She demonstrates on the basis of mortals' opinions that mortals' opinions are flawed.

Then the goddess's arguments do not establish that what-is is one and unchanging. Nor do they establish unequivocally or unproblematically that on a viable road of inquiry, we must say and conceive that it is that way. What they seem to reveal, and what their framing in the poem reflects, is that what inquiry and inference seem to require, given the opinions of mortals, is at odds with itself. I suggest that this is not a reason to abandon inquiry, and that Parmenides may not have thought it a reason to do so. Instead, it encourages us to acknowledge our linguistic and conceptual starting-points, and to strive to investigate their implications and limitations.

In order to live as humans, we evidently need to make inferences and choices.[29] Parmenides shows that from the standpoint of the assumptions we accept in order to live, those inferences and choices are at odds with themselves. To accept a principle of non-contradiction—as inquiry and choice seem to require—is simultaneously to deny that that principle can be completely realized in our opinions. To refer to what-is is to put ἀλήθεια out of reach. To be mortal, for Parmenides, is to journey through that incompleteness.

I hope I have been able to show that Parmenides was aware of the fact that everything he says, and everything we think in trying to understand it, is shot through with the opinions of mortals and thus riddled with liar paradoxes. I hope to have been a little convincing in showing that, given the opinions of mortals, the opinions of mortals and the way what-is is to be on the road of inquiry that the goddess recommends are symbiotic.

---

29   See Wians 2006.

PARMENIDES, LIARS, AND MORTAL INCOMPLETENESS

But if I have not been able to establish decisively that Parmenides would have seen these things, I hope to have shown that they are there for us to find. And I hope that finding them would be a way in which we could thank the ancient Greeks for enabling us to go this further step. I can see a number of ways in which recognizing this thoroughgoing paradoxicality of any system of identifications could challenge the hubris of all unconditional and direct claims about the nature of what-is, and thus bring us to open up dialogues across cultures and ways of knowledge.

I hope that seeing this paradoxicality will help us become more aware of the many ways in which inquiry toward our mortal notion of ἀλήθεια is worthwhile. We do not seem to be able to root out all of the flaws and tensions in the starting points and the tools of inquiry. But we would do well to begin the task of acknowledging the starting points and their flaws and tensions. And then if this return formed part of a journey that looped back and repeated, we could examine the beginnings and underpinnings of each of our inquiries, and the beginnings and underpinnings of those examinations, and so on—perhaps indefinitely.[30] This project puts us in touch continually both with our mortality, (our lack) and with that in the face of which it is mortality or lack. If ἀλήθεια requires that we try to confront distortion and gaps—and seek wholes and origins—this is the way, Parmenides suggests, to orient ourselves toward it. Failure to do this means that we consign to oblivion (opposite of ἀλήθεια) what custom does not acknowledge, and restrict the possibility of finding justice or knowledge.[31] The more contradictions and incoherences we confront, the more we support the hope that there is a basis for right and truth that is not arbitrary.[32]

---

30 Barrett 2004 and Miller 2006 have elaborated this account of the journey much more acutely and lucidly than I can hope to do.

31 On oblivion (λήθη) as opposite to ἀλήθεια, see the sources mentioned in note 19.

32 For their comments, suggestions and criticisms, all of which have improved this paper, I am indebted to the BACAP commentator, Yale Weiss; and to Wes DeMarco, Gary Gurtler, Daniel Maher, Max Latona, May Sim, and an anonymous reviewer for this publication. Remaining errors are my own.

COLLOQUIUM 1

Commentary on Cherubin

Yale Weiss
The Graduate Center, CUNY

Abstract

This commentary examines the interpretation of Parmenides developed by Rose Cherubin in her paper, "Parmenides, Liars, and Mortal Incompleteness." First, I discuss the tensions Cherubin identifies between the definitions and presuppositions of justice, necessity, fate, and the other requisites of inquiry. Second, I critically assess Cherubin's attribution of a sort of liar paradox to Parmenides. Finally, I argue that Cherubin's handling of the *Doxa*, the section of Parmenides' poem that deals with mortal opinion and cosmology, is unsatisfactory. I suggest that her reading may contradict the text in denying that the *Doxa* contains truths.

Keywords

Parmenides – Aletheia – Doxa – cosmology – inquiry

The fragments of Parmenides have inspired many disparate interpretations.[1] Most scholars have interpreted Parmenides as some sort of monist, be it numerical, predicational, generous, or material.[2] All monist interpretations are alike insofar as they see Parmenides' project as primarily oriented around describing reality, what-is. Moreover, such interpretations as a rule hold that Parmenides' poem contains truths about what-is and that the goddess of the poem proffers these.

By contrast, Cherubin advances an interpretation of Parmenides that sees him primarily concerned with what the requisites of inquiry (δίζησις) in accordance with ἀλήθεια are. In Cherubin's reading, Parmenides is the first philosopher for whom a certain type of meta-epistemic question arose. The question

---

1 This commentary was offered to the original version of "Parmenides, Liars, and Mortal Incompleteness" which has since been edited.

2 For an overview of these interpretations, see Sisko and Weiss 2015.

COMMENTARY ON CHERUBIN

is not that of *how* to get from point A to point B, but rather of *can* one get from point A to point B, from our present epistemic state to ἀλήθεια. The first is a distinctly methodological question, whereas the latter concerns the very possibility of inquiry.

For comparison, in the *Meno*, the possibility of *de novo* inquiry is threatened by a paradox which the theory of recollection is meant to respond to. Subsequently, the question of how to actually go about obtaining knowledge (is virtue teachable?) is answered with the method of hypothesis.[3]

Cherubin's Parmenides is concerned with the question of whether "mortal opinions [are] even such as to enable us to conceive and speak of what-is in a way that conduces to ἀλήθεια" (2018, 2). Can we mortals even conceptualize what-is in such a way that it is possible for us to engage in ἀλήθεια-yielding inquiry about it? Cherubin has Parmenides answer this question negatively, with certain caveats.

I want to examine three different aspects of Cherubin's interpretation in these comments. First, I discuss the tensions between the definitions and presuppositions of δίκη, ἀνάγκη, μοῖρα, and the other requisites of inquiry. Second, I assess Cherubin's attribution of a sort of liar paradox to Parmenides. Finally, I evaluate Cherubin's handling of the *Doxa*, the section of Parmenides' poem that deals with mortal opinion. I argue that it is unsatisfactory.

Cherubin defines a road of inquiry "as a series of oriented steps that one takes in inquiring" (2018, 4). It is necessary for being on such a road (that is, inquiring) that one be able to *recognize* what-is. To "seek salamanders, one needs to be able to identify which things are salamanders" (Cherubin 2018, 5).[4] Recognizing that you have found the thing being searched after essentially involves distinction and differentiation. Other requisites of inquiry—those associated with δίκη, ἀνάγκη, and μοῖρα —conflict with requisites like distinction and change.

The roles of δίκη, ἀνάγκη, and μοῖρα are spelled out in B8.1–49. Justice (δίκη) holds what-is fast, necessity (ἀνάγκη) holds it bound in a limit, and fate (μοῖρα) binds it to be whole and unchanging (B8.14, 30, 37). δίκη is construed as a condition of regularity and order on what-is (Cherubin 2018, 5, 6). Methods of inquiry like process of elimination require that the subject being investigated have stable characteristics by which it may be identified. For Cherubin's Parmenides, δίκη is a very stringent condition which is incompatible with the passage of time and change in the world.

---

3 See, e.g., Benson 2015, 51.

4 Compare with *Meno* 8od.

Consider, also, the case of μοῖρα. This is understood as (enforcing) a requirement that the whole of what-is and its relations be continuous (Cherubin 2018, 5). In the absence of this requirement, there would be relational gaps which would in turn result in explanatory and causal gaps and thwart inquiry; being unable to identify things (since identity is partly discerned through such relations), Cherubin suggests that inquiry could not even begin (2018, 8). But while μοῖρα keeps what-is *whole*, the notion invokes the concepts of share, portion, and part. Indeed, the word is often translated as such.

Cherubin is not the first to note the array of tensions in this part of Parmenides' poem, but the attention she gives to δίκη, ἀνάγκη, and μοῖρα in this respect is unusual and illuminating. Because Parmenides' work is a poem, there is perhaps a natural tendency towards deflating various tensions that arise from the language used in the section on truth. We excuse Parmenides for saying, in the same breath, that what-is is ἀκίνητον and that becoming and perishing have strayed away (B8.26–28). Cherubin has sought to magnify these sorts of tensions and understand them not as poetic license, but as an integral part of what she takes Parmenides' central project to be.

What *does* Cherubin take Parmenides' project to be? The arguments Parmenides gives concerning what-is are underpinned by a conceptual scheme of distinction, difference, and change, a scheme which finds expression in Parmenides' cosmology of Light and Night. That is, the coherence of the arguments—arguments which invoke the notions of change, difference, and negation—is predicated upon mortal opinions; and the arguments show those same mortal opinions to be flawed.

For Cherubin, this is not merely a *reductio ad absurdum*. Rather, it is a sort of liar paradox. As she puts it, "From the suppositions that make inquiry and inference possible, given my opinions as a mortal, it follows—I infer—that mortals' opinions undermine inference" (2018, 13). The sorts of concepts which ground inquiry (distinction, etc.) are what Parmenides' arguments concerning the requisites of inquiry show to be inconsistent with inquiry.

It bears emphasis that Cherubin is attributing a *sort of* liar paradox to Parmenides, rather than *the* liar paradox. She (at least initially) emphasizes that the argument reduces *terms* to absurdity (2018, 13). Since the heart of any liar paradox is a problem of truth, and this is a problem with the sense of terms, the attribution of a liar paradox would seem to be flawed. Perhaps more appositely, one can discern, as Owen famously did, certain figures of Wittgenstein's (rather than of Epimenides') in Parmenides.[5]

---

5 "His [Parmenides'] argument, to adopt an analogy of Sextus and Wittgenstein, is a ladder which must be thrown away when one has climbed it" (Owen 1960, 100).

COMMENTARY ON CHERUBIN

Cherubin's paradox is different in form from the liar and "does not turn entirely on truth-values" (2018, 13). While she gestures at ways of casting the paradox, she does not give the form or explain in what precise sense it is a relative of the liar. Perhaps she holds that formalization would be pointless or impossible given the inexactness of the operative notion of ἀλήθεια.

Finally, I want to discuss Cherubin's handling of the *Doxa*, the section of Parmenides' poem concerning natural philosophy. Long the most neglected part of Parmenides' work, it has recently become the subject of more serious scholarly attention, and deservedly so. It was, after all, most likely the longest part of Parmenides' poem and made serious original contributions to science (Sisko and Weiss 2015, 43).

The goddess explicitly indicates that it contains truths, or in any case things that can be known (see especially B10). It is largely for this reason that I would argue that no interpretation of Parmenides will suffice which denies legitimacy to the *Doxa*. On these grounds, numerical monist readings of Parmenides must be rejected. So too must Cherubin's interpretation. It will be profitable to explain why in some detail.

For Cherubin, the Light/Night scheme can play a role in articulating things that might be true or false—it provides a framework for articulating propositions and inquiring. Mortal opinion allows for "something that appears to work like explanation" (Cherubin 2018, 18). But Cherubin explicitly disavows that Parmenides' discoveries result in ἀλήθεια; rather, they "are explanations that have a certain kind of predictive success, or at very least descriptive and explanatory success" (2018, 18).

As Cherubin recognizes, attributing some notion of predictive success to Parmenides runs the risk of anachronism. She clarifies that Parmenides' scheme does not generate quantitative predictions or experimentally falsifiable hypotheses more generally (2018, 18). Nevertheless, Parmenides' scheme affords some sort of descriptive success and prediction of a limited kind.[6]

Even if it is granted that Parmenides' discussion of the opinions of mortals is oriented around giving an account which is predictively successful (broadly construed), a question remains about how to square this with his apparent (albeit qualified) attribution of veracity to his cosmology. If the κοῦρος is to come to know things about the cosmos, surely the goddess must be offering ἀλήθεια and not merely predictively useful falsities.

This objection can perhaps be sidestepped by arguing that ἀλήθεια is a stricter notion than truth. It is consistent for the goddess to offer knowledge

---

6   More specifically, certain of Parmenides' claims about Venus and the moon allow for limited sorts of prediction.

without offering ἀλήθεια if knowledge that *p* does not entail that *p* is ἀληθής. Thus, mortals' opinions could be accurate and true without giving ἀλήθεια (Cherubin 2018, 18n24). But then it must be argued that the goddess's offers of knowledge about the cosmos are not also offers of ἀλήθεια.

I have been citing the goddess's claims as evidence for there being ἀλήθεια in the *Doxa*. Cherubin, holding that the goddess is herself a sort of liar paradox,[7] might hold that these knowledge claims are not to be taken seriously. But if the goddess does not mean to convey ἀλήθεια through the *Doxa*, why does the *Doxa* even exist? For Cherubin, it illustrates how to account for observable phenomena in a way that produces descriptive success using the tools of the Light/Night scheme (2018, 19). I do not find the textual support for this interpretation to be especially compelling.[8]

I want to conclude with a remark on the place of Parmenides in the history of philosophy. If something along the lines of what Cherubin has proposed were correct, Parmenides would be without philosophical precedent, but he would also have clear intellectual heirs. Cherubin has singled out Aristotle in her discussion, but I think Plato is more appropriate. A recurring theme in the dialogues is the difficulty, even the impossibility, of mortals obtaining knowledge (about virtue, about piety, etc.). Plato, unlike Parmenides, ultimately claims that mortals can obtain ἀλήθεια, and outlines dialectic as the method for doing so. Here, then, is yet another way in which Plato can be seen as responding to Parmenides.

---

7 See Cherubin 2018, 14.

8 Incidentally, the most natural explanation for the predictive success of a theory is that the theory is approximately true. Thus, it must not only be argued that Parmenides is primarily concerned with predictive success in this section of the poem, but that he did not take predictive success to indicate truth (or, in any case, ἀλήθεια).

COLLOQUIUM 1

Cherubin/Weiss Bibliography

Austin, S. 1986. *Parmenides: Being, Bounds, and Logic*. New Haven: Yale University Press.

Barrett, J. 2004. Struggling with Parmenides. *Ancient Philosophy* 24: 267–91.

Benardete, S. 1998. "Night and Day, ...": Parmenides. *Mètis* 13.1: 193–225.

Benson, H. 2015. *Clitophon's Challenge: Dialectic in Plato's Meno, Phaedo, and Republic*. Oxford: Oxford University Press.

Bollack, J. 2006. *Parménide: de l'étant au monde*. Lagrasse: Verdier.

Cerri, G. 2008. Testimonianze e frammenti di scienza parmenidea. In *Parmenide Scienziato?*, eds. L. Rossetti and F. Marcacci, 83–90. Eleatica 1. Sankt Augustin: Academia Verlag.

Cherubin, R. 2001. Λέγειν, Νοεῖν, and Τὸ Ἐόν in Parmenides. *Ancient Philosophy* 21: 277–303.

Cherubin, R. 2005. Light, Night, and the Opinions of Mortals; Parmenides B8.51–61 and B9. *Ancient Philosophy* 25: 1–23.

Cherubin, R. 2009. *Alētheia* from Poetry into Philosophy: Homer to Parmenides. In *Logos and Muthos: Philosophical Essays in Greek Literature*, ed. W. Wians, 51–72. Albany: State University of New York Press.

Clark, S.R.L. 2008. Deconstructing the Laws of Logic. *Philosophy* 83: 25–53.

Cole, T. 1983. Archaic Truth. *Quaderni urbinati di cultura classica* 13: 7–28.

Collobert, C. 1993. *L'être de Parménide ou le refus du temps*. Paris: Kimé.

Constantineau, P. 1987. La question de la vérité chez Parménide. *Phoenix* 41: 217–240.

Coxon, A.H. 2009. *The Fragments of Parmenides: A Critical Text with Introduction and Translation, the Ancient Testimonia and a Commentary*, ed. R.D. McKirahan. Las Vegas: Parmenides Publishing.

Curd, P. 2004. *The Legacy of Parmenides: Eleatic Monism and Later Presocratic Thought*. Las Vegas: Parmenides Publishing.

Detienne, M. 1990. *Les Maîtres de vérité dans la Grèce archaïque*, rev. ed. Paris: Editions La Découverte.

Fränkel, H. 1960. Parmenidesstudien. In *Wege und Formen frühgriechischen Denkens*, 2nd ed., ed. F. Tietze, 157–197. Munich: Beck.

Gantz, T. 1996. *Early Greek Myth: A Guide to Literary and Artistic Sources*. Baltimore: Johns Hopkins University Press.

Germani, G. 1988. ΑΛΗΘΕΙΑ in Parmenide. *La parola del passato* 43: 177–206.

Graham, D.W. 2006. *Explaining the Cosmos: The Ionian Tradition of Scientific Philosophy*. Princeton: Princeton University Press.

Graham, D.W. 2013. *Science before Socrates: Parmenides, Anaxagoras, and the New Astronomy*. Oxford: Oxford University Press.

Henn, M. 2003. *Parmenides of Elea: A Verse Translation with Interpretative Essays and Commentary to the Text*. Westport: Praeger.

Hirzel, R. 1966. *Themis, Dike und Verwandtes*. Reprint. Hildesheim: Olms.

Murray, A.T., tr. 1919. *Homer, The Odyssey*. The Loeb Classical Library. Cambridge: Harvard University Press.

Jaeger, W., ed. 1957. *Aristotle, Metaphysica*. Oxford: Clarendon Press.

Journée, G. 2012. Lumière et Nuit, Féminin et Masculin chez Parménide d'Elée: quelques remarques. *Phronesis* 57: 289–318.

Krischer, T. 1965. ΕΤΥΜΟΣ und ΑΛΗΘΗΣ. *Philologus* 109: 161–174.

Levet, J.P. 1976. *Le vrai et le faux dans la pensée grecque archaïque*. Paris: Les Belles Lettres.

Lloyd-Jones, H. 1971. *The Justice of Zeus*. Berkeley and Los Angeles: University of California Press.

Long, A.A. 1975. The Principles of Parmenides' Cosmology. In *Studies in Presocratic Philosophy*, eds. R.E. Allen and D.J. Furley, vol. 2, 82–101. London and New York: Routledge & Kegan Paul.

Mansfeld, J. 1964. *Die Offenbarung des Parmenides und die menschliche Welt*. Assen: Van Gorcum.

Merlan, P. 1976. Neues Licht auf Parmenides. In *Kleine Philosophische Schriften*, ed. F. Merlan, 8–17. Hildesheim: Georg Olms Verlag.

Miller, M. 1979. Parmenides and the Disclosure of Being. *Apeiron* 13: 12–35.

Miller, M. 2001. 'First of all': On the Semantics and Ethics of Hesiod's Cosmogony. *Ancient Philosophy* 21: 251–275.

Miller, M. 2006. Ambiguity and Transport: Some Reflections on the Proem to Parmenides' Poem. *Oxford Studies in Ancient Philosophy* 30: 1–47.

Mourelatos, A.P.D. 2008. *The Route of Parmenides*. Rev. ed. Las Vegas: Parmenides Publishing.

Mourelatos, A.P.D. 2013. Parmenides, Early Greek Astronomy, and Modern Scientific Realism. In *Early Greek Philosophy: The Presocratics and the Emergence of Reason*, ed. J. McCoy, 91–112. Washington: Catholic University of America Press.

Onians, R.B. 1951. *The Origins of European Thought*. Cambridge: Cambridge University Press.

Owen, G.E.L. 1960. Eleatic Questions. *The Classical Quarterly* 10.1:84–102.

Popper, K.R. 1998. *The World of Parmenides: Essays on the Presocratic Enlightenment*, eds. A.F. Petersen and J. Mejer. London: Routledge.

Robbiano, C. 2006. *Becoming Being: On Parmenides' Transformative Philosophy*. International Pre-Platonic Studies 5. Sankt Augustin: Academia Verlag.

Rossetti, L. 2016. *Pseudophaēs* e *pseudophanēs*. La luna secondo Parmenide. In *Apis Matina: Studi in onore di Carlo Santini*, ed. A. Setaioli, 613–24. Trieste: EUT Edizioni Università di Trieste.

Schreckenberg, H. 1964. *Ananke: Untersuchungen zur Geschichte des Wortgebrauchs*. Munich: Beck.

Schürmann, R. 1996. *Des hégémonies brisées.* Mauvezin: Trans-Europ-Repress.

Sider, D., and H.W. Johnstone. 1986. *The Fragments of Parmenides*. Bryn Mawr Greek Commentaries. Bryn Mawr: Thomas Library, Bryn Mawr College.

Sisko, J.E., and Y. Weiss. 2015. A Fourth Alternative in Interpreting Parmenides. *Phronesis* 60: 40–59.

Stratton, G.M., ed. and tr. 1967. *Theophrastus and the Greek Physiological Psychology before Aristotle*. Reprint. Dubuque: W. Brown.

Tor, S. 2015. Parmenides' Epistemology and the Two Parts of His Poem. *Phronesis* 60: 3–39.

Vlastos, G. 1993. Equality and Justice in Early Greek Cosmologies. In *Studies in Greek Philosophy*, vol. 1, ed. D.W. Graham, 57–88. Princeton: Princeton University Press.

Wacziarg, A. 2008. For a rehabilitation of Parmenides' doxa. In *Parmenide Scienziato?*, eds. L. Rossetti and F. Marcacci, 143–151. Eleatica 1. Sankt Augustin: Academia Verlag.

Wians, W. 2006. The Philosopher's Knowledge of Non-Contradiction. *Ancient Philosophy* 26: 333–353.

COLLOQUIUM 2

The Metaphysics of the Syllogism

Edward C. Halper
University of Georgia

Abstract

This paper addresses a central metaphysical issue that has not been recognized: what kind of entity is a syllogism? I argue that the syllogism cannot be merely a mental entity. Some counterpart must exist in nature. A careful examination of the *Posterior Analytics*'s distinction between the syllogism of the fact and the syllogism of the reasoned fact shows that we must set aside contemporary logic to appreciate Aristotle's logic, enables us to understand the validity of the scientific syllogism through its content rather than its form, and explains the priority of the scientific syllogism over other valid syllogisms. The opening chapters of *Posterior Analytics* II help us to distinguish the entities that scientific syllogism must include as its terms; namely, a genus, an essential nature, and essential attributes of the genus. Often, the attributes are found in closely linked sequences. By exploring why there are such sequences and how they are linked, the paper argues that sequences of genus, nature, and sequential attributes are the basis in nature for the process of reasoning that we call the syllogism: we come to grasp the syllogism over time but the sequences to which it refers exist together in things. So understood, the syllogism, like knowledge of forms and truths, exists in us and in the world.

Keywords

syllogism – logic – validity – scientific syllogism – essential nature – essential attributes

I

Ancient philosophy has been so intensely studied for so long that it seems unlikely that any major issue remains unexplored. It will, therefore, come as something of a surprise to realize that the issue I will discuss here is not just unexplored by contemporary scholars but wholly unrecognized, even in passing. The issue can be stated simply: What is an Aristotelian syllogism? Of

© KONINKLIJKE BRILL NV, LEIDEN, 2018 | DOI 10.1163/22134417-00331P05

course, there has been a great deal of discussion of the syllogistic forms and especially of how to represent them in a formal deductive system. My question is ontological: what sort of entity is the syllogism?

Aristotle defines the syllogism as "a discourse (*logos*) in which certain things being stated, something other than what is stated follows of necessity, from their being so" (*Prior Analytics* I 1, 24b18–20, Jenkinson translation). Aristotle goes on to explain that what is "stated" are two premises that contain three terms and that what "follows of necessity" is a conclusion that contains two of these terms. (Although he uses "syllogism" to signify only valid syllogisms, the *Prior Analytics* considers all possible syllogistic forms in order to determine which are valid. Hence, it is more convenient to use "syllogism" to refer to the form, regardless of its validity.)

The Greek word that is here rendered "discourse," *logos,* could as well be understood as "process of reasoning." In any case, Aristotle's definition is notably opaque on what the syllogism is, on why a conclusion would follow from what is posited, and on why the inference would be necessary.

Contrast Aristotle's definition of a (valid) syllogism with his account of true propositions:

> An affirmation is a positive assertion of something about something, a denial a negative assertion. It is possible to assert of what holds that it does not hold and of what does not hold that it does, as well as to assert of what holds that it does hold and of what does not hold that it does not. (*De Interpretatione* 6, 17a25–29, my translation)

Propositions are true when they express what holds in the world. A valid syllogism, that is, a "perfect syllogism" needs "nothing other than what has been stated to make plain what necessarily follows" (*APr.* 24b22–25, Jenkinson translation). Whereas something in the world makes a proposition true, a syllogism is recognized as valid from itself, independently of anything in the world.

Nonetheless, the syllogism is used to draw inferences about the world. Why does a valid syllogism whose premises are true yield a conclusion that is also true? Inasmuch as the syllogism is a tool for deriving or, at least, affirming some truths about the world on the basis of others, the assertions that constitute a sound syllogism must be linked together somehow not only in our minds, but also in the world. What is it in the world that allows a syllogism whose premises are true to yield a true conclusion? Again, a syllogism that was merely valid might, conceivably, lack a connection with the world, but it is impossible to suppose that a *sound* syllogism would not have something in the world that would somehow correspond to it. This something must be more than whatever

THE METAPHYSICS OF THE SYLLOGISM   33

it is that corresponds to the sound syllogism's three propositions, for their very
connection in the syllogism signifies something about the world: three true
sentences need not be a syllogism. My concern here is what this could be.
Thus, to ask "what is a syllogism?" in the way I am proposing here, is to ask,
"what is it *in the world* that corresponds with and, thereby, legitimates a sound
Aristotelian syllogism?" Why can we assume that a *logos* that we can recognize
to be valid only from what it states also applies to the world? Inasmuch as the
Posterior Anyalytics aims to show how to use the syllogism to arrive at scientific knowledge of the world, my question is crucial for understanding this
work.

Again, a *logos* is either a series of sentences or a process of reasoning. Maybe
it would not be too surprising if there were some pattern in the sentences or in
the reasoning to which our human intellect must somehow give its assent. The
primary rule of inference in contemporary logic, *modus ponens*, may be just
such a pattern. What is difficult to understand is why such a pattern, process of
reasoning, or discourse—or whatever else it might be—must also hold of the
world. Why can reasoning about the world be a way to discover what is true of
the world?

Someone might think this question could be answered by identifying "truthmakers" in the world that make each premise of a valid syllogism true and then
by showing that they *imply* a third truthmaker that makes the conclusion true.
The issue is what sort of thing in the world this implication would be. Since
merely being true does not suffice for three sentences to constitute a syllogism,
there must be something in the world besides the three truthmakers that
somehow makes them into a syllogism. What could this be? To coin a term,
what is the "soundness maker"? This is the question I am posing here.

In short, to ask, "what is a syllogism?" in the way I am proposing here is to
ask, "what is it *in the world* that constitutes the peculiar process of inference
that is an Aristotelian syllogism?" Can processes of inference exist in the world
or is there, rather, something else in the world that allows there to be sound
mental *inference*? So understood, the question is about the relation of logic to
the world. This was once a central question for philosophers. In the *Tractatus*
Wittgenstein understands the structure of logic as the structure of the world as
well as the structure of language; in his later work, logic comes to be a collection of grammatical features of our language, features we often find useful—
though not always, as Graham Priest likes to remind us.[1] Even if we had no
other reason to raise the question, it would be interesting to inquire into how
Aristotle understands his logic to relate to the world.

---

1   In multiple books and articles. See, for example, Priest 2006.

II

In fact, though, we have good reasons from Aristotle's philosophy to raise this question. In the *De Anima* Aristotle maintains that the form that is a thing's essential nature exists both in the thing and in the mind, albeit in the former with matter and in the latter without (III 4, 429a13–18). In this respect, the intelligible form parallels the sensible form that exists in an object and in the pertinent sense organ of the sensing animal. In other words, the essential nature that we know also exists, albeit with matter, in the thing known. The existence of this nature in our minds is necessary if we are to know the object, Aristotle maintains. Were our minds to have an image or representation of the object, we would not have knowledge; nor would we have real knowledge if we grasped the object by somehow sending out a beam of light or something else, as bats grasp the world, and as Plato seems to think we sense (*Timaeus* 45c).

The paradigmatic essential natures that we know are the essential natures of substances. But there is no reason to suppose that only substances have essential natures: Aristotle speaks of knowledge of: mathematical entities (quantities) (*Metaphysics* K 3, 1061a28–b3), colors (*Metaph.* I 7, 1057a18–b34; *De Sensu* 3), and grammar (*Categories* 1a29–b3). Indeed, in the *Metaphysics* he claims that substances have essences most properly, but that instances of other categories have essences as well, albeit derivatively (Z 4, 1030a38–32). Importantly, for us, the *Metaphysics* makes clear that something's essential attributes have their own essences, though, again, not in the primary way: "in one way there will not be definitions or essences of anything except substances, but in another way there will be" (Z 5, 1031a1–14).[2] Aristotle claims here that the essential attributes have essences "by addition." What this means becomes clear when the *Posterior Analytics* discusses essential attributes in chapter 4 of book I. Attributes are essential to some subject, first, when the subject is included in the formula that makes clear what the attribute is; thus, the definition of odd includes number (the example also appears in the passage just cited from *Metaph.* Z 5) and the definition of straight includes line (73a37–b3; *Metaph.* 1031a1–5). That is to say, the essential definition of straight does not express an independent, self-subsistent entity. Since straight does not exist without a line in which it inheres, the essential nature of straight includes the essential nature of line "by addition," as the *Metaphysics* puts it. My point here is that these passages make clear that an essential attribute *has* an essential *nature*. Like the line in which straight inheres and the sensible substance in

---

2 See Halper 2005, 71–72.

THE METAPHYSICS OF THE SYLLOGISM

which the line inheres, straight is a form that can exist in the world and, when it is known, in our minds.

Posterior Analytics I 4 describes another kind of essential attribute that is important for demonstrative knowledge: the essential attributes that are included within the essential definition of some subject (I 4, 73a34–37). Once again, Aristotle's examples of these attributes include the line, but now it is an attribute of the triangle because it is included within the definition of the triangle. Since we know that line has an essential nature because it is an essential attribute inhering in a substance (that is, since it is the first sort of essential attribute), it is clear that line and the other attributes that are essential because they are included in an essential definition (that is, since they are the second sort of essential attribute) must also have their own essential natures. It is important that the definitions of essential attributes are intrinsically linked to the natures to which they belong because it is these two types of essential attributes that can be demonstrated (I 22, 84a11–17). We will come back to this link later.

The essential natures of substances and their essential attributes are among the terms of scientific syllogisms. There is another thing that can appear as a term in a syllogism: a genus or a species (I 7, 75a42–b2). These usually serve as the subjects whose attributes are demonstrated, and they are universals. The last chapter of the *Posterior Analytics* claims that we can come to know a universal through repeated sensation. Eventually, the sensible's features "take a stand" like soldiers who stem a rout in battle when they turn around and the battle lines reform around them, and we can identify a universal character that a group of sensibles share (II 19, 100a3–b5). The universal here seems to be an identifying character that enables us to say that something is, say, a man or a dog. Interestingly, some *sensible* feature common to a class of individuals somehow comes to exist in the *mind* as the character that is common to all instances of the genus. What makes a character that can be *sensed* into something that is grasped by *reason*? Apparently, it is just its being able to be used to mark off a class of things.

The generic character that we use to designate a class is just one of multiple characteristics that are common to the class. Presumably, we come to know these characters by the same sort of induction from sensible instances. Those universal characters we see first are "prior to us" but not "prior in nature" (I 2, 71b33–72a5). The essential nature of the class is prior in nature, and it accounts, somehow, for the other characters that are common to the class.

Aristotle's point is that after the repeated sensations of similar objects, we somehow grasp a feature or features that mark off things as being of a single type, a genus. This same sort of repeated sensation allows us to recognize other features of the genus, such as "having two legs" or "the capacity to laugh." Once we have identified a group of such characters that are common to the genus, we can ask which of them is the essential nature that defines it. One sign of the essential nature is that the other characters common to the genus can be understood to belong to the genus in respect of this nature. As I said, this essential nature exists both in the things included within the genus and in the mind that grasps this nature. Again, if the essential nature has this dual existence, then so, too, must those universals that initially come to be grasped through sensation; namely, the genus and all its essential attributes. If the form that is sensed exists in the thing and in a sense organ, then the universals that result when sensations "take a stand" must also exist in the things, somehow, and in the mind. In sum, *all* three terms of the syllogism exist in things and, equally, in the mind.

If the terms that are contained in the syllogism exist in things, must not the inference between them that constitutes the syllogism also exist in things? Can a syllogism be merely a mental addition to the physical counterparts of the individual terms? Surely, there must be something in the things corresponding to the inference, something in the things that corresponds to the syllogism as a whole, or possibly both. If a form that is known exists in the mind and in the thing and if a true proposition with this form exists in the mind and, somehow, in things, then the scientific knowledge, that is, the knowledge through the syllogism that demonstrates the proposition must also exist in the mind and, somehow, in things.

III

In order to pursue our problem, we need to appreciate Aristotle's account of the scientific syllogism. Aristotle gives an account of the syllogism in general in the *Prior Analytics*. He is particularly concerned with setting out the three figures and showing which *forms* are valid. The *Prior Analytics* is Aristotle's formal logic. (A number of readers have tried to put Aristotle's account into the formal logic that is in wide use today.) In the *Posterior Analytics* Aristotle expounds the *scientific* syllogism. Two syllogistic forms could be scientific syllogisms, one positive and the other negative, but the more important of these is the positive form, and it is the form that Aristotle usually uses to express a scientific syllogism. This form was called by the medieval mnemonic, "Barbara":

$$\text{All B is C}$$
$$\underline{\text{All A is B}}$$
$$\therefore \ \text{All A is C}$$

THE METAPHYSICS OF THE SYLLOGISM   37

The other form of a scientific syllogism was called "Celarent":

No B is C
All A is B
∴ No A is C

Both are clearly valid syllogistic forms, but it is not merely its form that makes
a syllogism scientific. It must also meet various criteria that the *Posterior Analytics* specifies: Its premises must be true, primary, immediate, and the premises must also be more known than, prior to, and the causes of their conclusions
(71b19–22). The assumption is that only what cannot be otherwise can be
known (71b12). In order that the syllogism be able to convey scientific knowledge (ἐπιστήμη), that is, demonstrative knowledge, what its premises affirm or
deny cannot be otherwise and so, consequently, what its conclusion affirms or
denies cannot be otherwise. Hence, the scientific syllogism must have necessary premises and conclusion (71b12–16). Moreover, that "through which" some
attribute C belongs (or does not belong) to the subject A must itself belong to
the subject "more" (72a28–29). In other words, the cause of the subject's having
or not having an attribute, the attribution that the conclusion asserts or denies,
is a middle term whose own attribution to the subject is prior to that of the attribute. Importantly, Aristotle calls such a middle term the "cause" (90a5–7).
A syllogism that meets these criteria is "scientific" or, equivalently, it constitutes demonstrative knowledge. (Although they are often called "explanatory
syllogisms," this phrase captures neither the scientific syllogism's demonstrative necessity nor the *essential* priority of its middle term.)

These criteria are widely understood to specify *additional* conditions that
make a valid syllogism scientific. Thus, they are taken to be grafted on to syllogistic forms that are recognizably valid. I am going to challenge this view, but
first we need to see why it seems plausible and, in the process, come to appreciate how these criteria actually work.

One place where they do *seem*, at least at first, to be grafted on to the syllogistic form is Aristotle's important distinction between the "syllogism of the
fact" (τὸν τοῦ ὅτι συλλογισμόν) and the "syllogism of the reasoned fact" (τὸν τοῦ
διότι συλλογισμόν) in I 13 (see 78b32–34, 78a36–37). Both are valid syllogisms,
but they differ "according to the position of the middle terms." In the syllogism
of the reasoned fact, the causal term appears as the middle term. In the syllogism of the fact, this causal term occupies another position, out of place, as it
were. Aristotle's illustrations are memorable:

1. Whatever is not-twinkling is near.
   <u>All the planets are not-twinkling.</u>
   ∴ All the planets are near.

2. Whatever is near is not-twinkling.
   <u>All the planets are near.</u>
   ∴ All the planets are not-twinkling.

Both syllogisms are formally valid, but the first, the syllogism of the fact, puts "not-twinkling" in the middle position. If this syllogism were a scientific syllogism, "not-twinkling" would belong to the planets "more" than being near and, thereby, be the cause of the planets' being near. In other words, syllogism would claim that the planets are near *because* they are not-twinkling. The second syllogism is the syllogism of the reasoned fact because it rightly uses the nearness of the planets to explain their not-twinkling (78a36–38).

Aristotle does not explain how we know that it is the planets' nearness that causes them not to twinkle, rather than their not-twinkling that causes them to be near. He relies on our ordinary experiences of objects that are relatively near: they do not twinkle (78a34–35). But this observation supports the first premises of both syllogisms equally. We also need to recognize that to say that the planets are near is to express how they are, whereas to say that they do not twinkle is to express how they appear. That the way things are accounts for their appearances, rather than the other way around, is assumed here as an axiom. Like the principle of non-contradiction, which is assumed in every syllogism, the priority of being to appearance is assumed without being stated (compare I 11, 77a10–12, 27–28). Recognizing the axiom, we can see that 2, rather than 1, is the syllogism of the reasoned fact. But Aristotle does not invoke this axiom even here; he simply asserts that twinkling is not the cause of nearness (78a36–38). Clearly, we would not be able to rely on this or, perhaps, any other axiom to distinguish every syllogism of the reasoned fact. Rather, Aristotle seems to suppose that we simply have an innately human ability to discern that one thing is a cause and another is not. This ability is necessary to have demonstrative knowledge.[3]

---

3   Bronstein 2016 claims that we recognize that syllogism 2 is the syllogism of the reasoned fact from some prior knowledge; in particular, (a) by knowing noetically that "all planets are near" is a first principle and, thus, that syllogism 1 cannot demonstrate it or (b) by having demonstrations of both premises of syllogism 2. However, so far from taking "all planets are near" to be known noetically, I 13 claims that "planets are not twinkling" is "more known" (78a26–32). Aristotle means, of course, "more known to us." The point is that even though noetic knowledge is immediate in itself, we do not have it immediately and Aristotle does not assume it in

THE METAPHYSICS OF THE SYLLOGISM   39

As I said, this I 13 passage *seems* to support the idea that the demonstrative syllogism is just a syllogism with extra conditions because the syllogism of the fact and the syllogism of the reasoned fact, 1 and 2, have the same syllogistic form and differ only in that the middle term of syllogism 2 is a cause, whereas the middle term of 1 is not. More precisely, the conditions of the priority of the premises to the conclusion for scientific knowledge (ἐπιστήμη), spelled out in I 2 (71b9–19) are met by syllogism 2, but not by syllogism 1.

The question I want to raise is whether the causal role of the middle term in the syllogism of the reasoned fact is an additional condition that can be readily grafted onto the account of the syllogism in the *Prior Analytics* or whether it fundamentally transforms the syllogism so that it can serve as the expression of demonstrative knowledge. In the latter case, the syllogism of the *Prior Analytics* would play a heuristic role in uncovering the scientific knowledge expressed only in a syllogism of the reasoned fact. In this way, scientific knowledge would emerge as the unifying goal of both *Analytics*.

We are in nearly uncharted territory here, and it is only fair to warn the reader that what follows will prove challenging; indeed, all the more so to readers familiar with contemporary logic. As Jonathan Barnes noted, both syllogisms "would count as explanatory on the orthodox modern account of explanation" because on the "Human notion of causation" that is "a presupposition of that account, ... the major premises of both accounts are equally causal."[4] Barnes claims that Aristotle does not explain why non-twinkling can be "explained" by nearness, but not the other way around, until he discusses essence in *Posterior Analytics* II (16, 98b21-24). As we saw, I 13 treats the causal

---

I 13. In contrast, he does assume that "Whatever is not-twinkling is near" and "All the planets are not-twinkling" are both known immediately to perception (compare 78a34–35). As for Bronstein's (b), we do have a demonstration of one premise of syllogism 2, "all planets are near"; namely, syllogism 1. (The other premise is true by induction from sense perception.) But this demonstration implies that syllogism 1 is prior to syllogism 2, just the opposite of what Aristotle is arguing. The point Aristotle makes is that if there *are* demonstrations of a syllogism's premises, it cannot be the syllogism of the reasoned fact because it does not contain the first cause, which is a necessary requirement for being a syllogism of the reasoned fact (78a23–26). This is just the opposite of what Bronstein claims. Indeed, Bronstein seems to confuse Aristotle's discussion of two ways in which a syllogism would be a syllogism of the fact (78a23–36) with an account of how a syllogism could be recognized as a syllogism of the reasoned fact. Significantly, though, Aristotle just declares 2 to be the latter "since it is not that they are near because they do not twinkle, but that they do not twinkle because they are near" (78a36–37). That is to say, Aristotle takes the causal role of the planets' nearness to be obvious. Syllogism 2 is the syllogism of the reasoned fact because it has the cause in the causal, middle position.

4   Barnes 1993, 156.

priority of nearness to twinkling as obvious; II 16 does not justify this priority, but does indicate the basis for any causal priority. We will consider it shortly. First, though, notice how deeply insightful Barnes's words are, even if he himself does not always appreciate them.[5] We can appreciate the distinction between the syllogism of the fact and the syllogism of the reasoned fact by reflecting further on contemporary notions of logic. It is customary to refer to logic as "formal logic" by which we mean that a deduction, such as $p \supset q, p \vdash q$, holds whatever the values of p and q. Contemporary logicians rarely if ever consider the values of terms or whether there might be some values that would undermine or transform the inference. The conditional $p \supset q$ is now universally taken to be the so-called "material conditional": its truth value depends solely on the truth value of p and the truth value of q. No connection between p and q is assumed. So, no one objects to a conditional like "if 2+3=5, then π is the ratio of the circumference of a circle to its radius" or questions its truth. Nor is there much concern that a conditional in which the terms were intrinsically connected, like "if x>3 then x>2," would not be a material conditional. Some logicians have spoken of the "strict conditional" to mark the connection, but it is not widely used because the material condition has seemed to serve adequately to express conditionals with connected components or, at least, to express their truth conditions. As Barnes sees, the metaphysics of the material conditional is rooted in Hume's analysis of causality: Hume challenges his readers to find something in one sense perception that would necessarily connect it with a sense impression that succeeds it. Failing to find any such perception, he reduces causality to one type of perception's regularly following another type, that is, to the relation expressed by the material conditional. The early Wittgenstein and Russell expounded a metaphysics of logical atomism based on what they took to be presuppositions of logic. This metaphysics faded long ago, and today's logicians are apt to suppose that logic makes no metaphysical assumptions because it can be used to express everything or, at least, everything scientific.

---

5   Elsewhere he famously declares that the *Posterior Analytics* "attempt[s] to characterize and investigate an axiomatic deductive system," Barnes 1975, 87. Later, Barnes 1981, 33–34, cf. 30, claims that the *Posterior Analytics*'s theory of demonstration does not rely on the theory of syllogistic in the *Prior Analytics*. He argues for the *chronological* priority of the account of demonstration, suggests that non-syllogistic demonstration is important for Aristotelian science (whereas syllogistic is not), and speculates (contrary to I 14 and most of book II) that Aristotle was "never in a position to assess" the application of syllogism to demonstration (59). Ultimately, though, he thinks an Aristotelian science is a "coherent sequence of propositions" deduced from primary propositions (27). Despite recognizing important differences between contemporary logic and Aristotle's logic, he continued to represent the latter by means of the former.

THE METAPHYSICS OF THE SYLLOGISM   41

These reflections on contemporary logic have no direct bearing on Aristotle's understanding of the syllogism, but I think they help to explain why readers have tended to think of the syllogism of the reasoned fact as a syllogism of the fact with some added conditions. Formally, the syllogism of the fact and the syllogism of the reasoned fact are identical. Both are composed of three terms that are extensionally identical. It makes no difference formally which position any of the terms occupies. Both syllogisms are equally valid. If Aristotle prefers one set of positions to another, it can only be for reasons that are extraneous to the syllogism itself. Or so it has seemed.

We have only to set aside (1) Humean causality along with the notions that (2) inference must be only formal and that (3) inference is justified extensionally to let the Aristotelian picture emerge from I 13. (1) We have seen that in a scientific syllogism, Aristotle claims the middle term is a cause, specifically, the cause of some attribute's necessarily belonging to a subject. This cause is not a Humean regular conjunction because mere conjunction could never be necessary. It should not be surprising that Aristotle's causes are pre-Humean. Only one of the terms of the syllogism is properly causal because, as we have seen, this term belongs to the subject term "more" than the other and because this other term somehow belongs to the subject *because* it belongs to the middle term. Only one of the three terms is properly a subject: it either is a substance or can be treated as a substance (that is, as if it were separate, compare *Metaph.* M 3, 1078a17–21). (2) Whereas contemporary logic is formal insofar as the content of its propositions or its predicates is irrelevant to logical truth, Aristotle insists that the proper term must occupy the middle position if there is to be a scientific syllogism. Again, truths of contemporary logic do not depend on what the p's and q's signify, whereas the content of the B term in the Barbara syllogism is critical if the syllogism is to be scientific. (3) Inasmuch as the syllogism of the fact and the syllogism of the reasoned fact are both valid because their terms have the same extensions, the difference between them cannot arise from their extensions. If, then, the one syllogism constitutes scientific knowledge whereas the other does not, scientific knowledge cannot come from grasping that a syllogism is valid through its extension. Since the middle term is the cause and since it must occupy the B position to make clear that it is through it that C belongs to A, it is clear that we grasp the truth of the conclusion of a scientific syllogism through the one term that can exclusively serve as its cause. However, to say that the truth of the conclusion follows from a single, specific causal term is to deny that the conclusion follows merely from the extension of the terms! Whereas the truth of the conclusion of a syllogism of the fact follows from the common *extensions* of its three terms, the truth of the conclusion of a syllogism of the reasoned fact follows from the particular natures of those terms, that is, from their intensions or, more specifically, from the intension of the middle term. Equivalently, since the *Prior Analytics* catalogues a number of syllogistic forms that are valid when all three terms have the same extensions, we can say that the syllogism of the fact is valid because of its form, whereas the syllogism of the reasoned fact is valid because of its content. Of course, the syllogism of the reasoned fact is also valid because of its form, but this form, which it shares with the syllogism of the fact is not what makes it scientific knowledge. Rather, we have scientific knowledge when we know a conclusion through its cause, and the syllogism of the reasoned fact shows how that is possible. But the conclusion has to be known *through its cause*, not through its syllogistic form or through a shared extension, and to know it through its cause is to know the conclusion through the special nature or meaning of the syllogism's B term. It is evident that to know a conclusion scientifically is the highest way it can be known (ἐπιστήμη), short of some sort of direct vision (νοῦς). Grasping a conclusion through a syllogism of the fact is a much weaker type of knowledge, barely deserving of being called knowledge at all.

Yet, I 13 suggests that if we can attain syllogism of the fact, we may be able to transform it into a syllogism of the reasoned fact by rearranging its terms. Thus, the elaborate account of valid syllogistic forms that occupies the *Prior Analytics* can be seen to serve a propaedeutic to the inquiry into the causes that is central to the *Posterior Analytics*. The syllogistic serves as a tool to help uncover terms that are properly causal and, thereby, the key constituents of scientific knowledge. However, it is only the scientific syllogism that counts as scientific knowledge because it alone is a way of knowing something through its cause (compare *Metaph.* A 3, 984a24–26). Since it is this cause rather than the syllogistic form that makes the conclusion of the scientific syllogism true, it is the basis of the validity of the scientific syllogism.

The notion that there are two possible sources of validity of a syllogism, its content or its form, has no counterpart in contemporary logic where content plays no role. Hence, it will not sit well with contemporary readers. Moreover, it is indeed puzzling how the same syllogism can be valid both because of its form and because of its content. I think that the root of the problem is the supposition that the syllogism of the fact and the syllogism of the reasoned fact are both syllogisms and that their differences must be somewhat superficial because both have the same syllogistic form. My strategy has been to show that their differences are significant, so significant, I now suggest, as to make them distinct entities. A syllogism of the fact can only rely on its form for its validity because the terms need share only common extension. To be sure, usually the terms in a valid syllogism of the fact will also share common content, but we

THE METAPHYSICS OF THE SYLLOGISM   43

do not need to use this content because we can draw the conclusion from its form alone. Indeed, since Aristotle assumes that whenever two characters are always present together, they must be essentially connected, there will *always* be common content among the terms of a syllogism of the fact. That makes the syllogism of the fact a useful step in the discovery of this connection. In contrast, a syllogism of the reasoned fact is valid because of the content of its terms, not because of its form. However, content that functions causally naturally takes the form of the Barbara syllogism because there the real cause is positioned so as to serve as the cause. Ironically, then, the syllogism of the reasoned fact takes on the same form as the Barbara syllogism of the fact, yet its validity does not stem from this form. It is clear that the meaning of validity differs in the two types of syllogism, for a syllogism of the fact is valid insofar as its conclusion follows from its premises by virtue of their common extension, whereas a syllogism of the reasoned fact is valid because its conclusion follows from the essential natures of the terms in its premises.

What difference could it make how or why a valid syllogism is valid? Is a syllogism more or less valid if it has a single source of validity or multiple sources of validity? Of course not. However, a syllogism whose validity depends on the nature of its terms has an intrinsic and necessary connection among these terms that the syllogism depending only on extension cannot have. In consequence, the conclusion of the syllogism of the reasoned fact is necessary and that of the syllogism of the fact is not. So, the source of validity makes a difference to the strength of the reasoning and the modality of the conclusion.

There is some small support for this interpretation in the next chapter, I 14. There Aristotle argues that the first figure is the most scientific. One reason is that it is the syllogism of the reasoned fact (79a17–24). He means, I think, that in the first figure the real cause of the thing stands in the causal position in the syllogism. That is to say, the cause is positioned in between the inner and outer terms, and it serves to link them together: in syllogism 2 above, the planets are non-twinkling *because* of their nearness. Here, the syllogistic form is perfectly suited to the content: it makes manifest the relation that the terms have in respect of their content. In contrast, the syllogism of the fact (1 above), has exactly the same syllogistic form, but its terms are not linked together by their content because there the middle term is not truly causal. The syllogism of the fact can only rely on its form for its validity.

A second reason that I 14 advances for the first syllogistic figure's being most scientific is that it enables us to pursue knowledge of the essence (79a24–25). This essence (B) is the cause of an attribute (C) belonging to a subject (A). Of course, the syllogism in the first figure need not have the essence in the proper position to be valid, but its terms can be rearranged to help us discover the essence, as I said. I 14's final reason for the first figure's being most scientific is that it can stand alone whereas instances of the other figures are shown to be valid or invalid by converting them into the first figure (79a29–32). This is a good summary of the procedure of the *Prior Analytics*. Aristotle evaluates the validity of syllogisms in the second and third figures by reducing them to syllogisms in the first figure. Further, he evaluates the validity of syllogisms in the first figure by reducing them to one of the two primary syllogisms, Barbara or Celarent. These are the instances of the first figure that properly stand alone. Why can Aristotle simply assume that they are valid? Perhaps, we can intuit their validity. However, as I 14's first reason suggests, in the syllogism of the reasoned fact, a syllogism that is always in the first figure, the middle term plays a causal role because it is located between the other two terms. As we saw, the syllogism of the reasoned fact is valid through its content, but that content properly takes on the form of a primary syllogism, Barbara. In this ideal case, the form of Barbara is a valid syllogistic form because of its content, but the form remains valid even when the content is not causal, albeit valid in a lesser way, as I have explained. Similarly, Celarent can be a valid syllogistic form because of its causal content inasmuch as the essence that occupies its middle position causes the subject not to have attributes that belong to an entirely distinct genus, and this syllogistic form remains valid, but only extensionally, when the middle term is not causal. My suggestion is that the properly causal roles of the content of Barbara and Celarent account for their strict, necessary validity and allow us to recognize the extensional validity of these forms even without their causal content. If, then, the *Prior Analytics* shows all the other syllogisms to depend on these, and these, in turn depend on scientific syllogisms that are valid through their content, then the entire syllogistic depends upon the causal essences necessary for scientific syllogisms.

From another point of view, we can say that this syllogistic leads us toward these essences. Early in the *Posterior Analytics* Aristotle distinguishes what is prior to us from what is prior in nature (I 2, 71b33–72a4). Although we must start with the former, we aim to arrive at the latter. This is what I think he did. The variety of syllogistic forms is what we notice first; it is prior to us. Some of these forms can be reduced to valid forms that are prior in nature, and these forms, in turn, reflect the material content of scientific syllogisms.[6]

In sum, my case for the priority of content validity rests on three arguments: (1) I 14's claim that the first figure is more scientific because it is the form of the

---

6 Goldin 2009 proposes a similar relation between the two works, but he claims, rightly, that the *Prior Analytics* provides matter for the *Posterior Analytics* form. I have reversed form and matter in order to compare Aristotle's syllogistic with contemporary logic.

THE METAPHYSICS OF THE SYLLOGISM 45

syllogism of the reasoned fact; (2) the same chapter's claim that the first figure is more scientific because it can stand alone; and (3) Aristotle's claim that what is "prior to us" is "posterior in nature" along with the recognition that the *Prior Analytics*'s exploration of extensional validity is prior to us.

There is a fourth reason for recognizing the priority of content validity. We saw at the beginning that the definition of a subject contains one type of essential attribute and that the definition of a second type of essential attribute contains its subject. Either definition can serve as the middle terms in a demonstration that essential attributes belong to a subject (II 16, 98b21–24). Such a syllogism links subject and attribute *through their natures*. It is, first and foremost, the essences of the terms that make the syllogism valid. As we saw, the syllogistic form can, at best, make this content validity apparent.

As I mentioned earlier, contemporary logic countenances only formal, extensional validity. To those schooled only in contemporary logic, the idea that logic might not be "formal logic" but rooted in the natures of things—what we could call, to make a contrast, "material logic"—is apt to seem entirely bizarre. My claim is that although Aristotle devotes the whole of the *Prior Analytics* to elucidating valid *forms* of inference, this entire account is "prior to us," whereas the account of scientific syllogism is "prior in nature." Scientific syllogisms have valid forms, but those forms are valid because of the nature of the terms and their relation to each other. That is why the *Prior Analytics* shows various syllogistic forms to be valid by reducing them to the Barbara syllogism of the first figure or to Celarent, the two syllogistic forms that reflect the material content of their terms. In the scientific syllogism, validity is a function of the content of the terms. Other syllogisms are valid, but only extensionally valid, because they have forms that are equivalent to the forms of syllogisms valid by their content. This extensional validity is, however, prior to us, and we can use it to discover the natures that are causes. If this is right, Aristotle's logic is indeed, an *organon*, a tool for discovering causal essential natures.

This account differs radically from standard readings of the text, and a brief paper can hardly be convincing. What I can do here is introduce this account and, thereby, raise the possibility of an alternative to the standard readings. One virtue of my reading is that it enables us to see the otherwise difficult and dry *Posterior Analytics* to be engaged in an exciting project, namely, explaining what the world must be like if it is to be known through demonstration. Not surprisingly, this project is closely connected with the central question of this paper, how the syllogism exists in the world. Instead of arguing further for content validity, let us turn to its consequences for our question. The first step is to appreciate just what the terms of the scientific syllogism are.

IV

Just what sort of thing is the causal middle term that plays so central a role in the scientific syllogism? In II 11, Aristotle insists that any of the four causes could be the middle term. However, his examples are not all scientific syllogisms. As usual in Aristotle, it is more important to look for the primary kind rather than the broad range of possibilities.

What the primary cause of the scientific syllogism is becomes clear at the beginning of book II. This book opens by distinguishing four types of things about which we inquire and, accordingly, four scientific questions: is it? (εἰ ἔστι), what is it? (τί ἔστιν), does P belong to S? (τὸ ὅτι), and why does P belong to S (τὸ διότι) (1, 89b23–25). These questions, he claims further, turn on two questions, is there a middle term in a syllogism? and what is this middle term? Scholars have wrestled with the question of how there could be a syllogism involved in either of the first two questions since they ask only about a single term, but I have argued elsewhere that Aristotle's point must be that we cannot ask about a single term without supposing some other character.[7] Hence, even if the question seems to be about a single term, it will be pursued along with some other term, and the inquiry will seek a middle term between them. It cannot be accidental that the Greek for "fact" and "reasoned fact" in the "syllogism of the fact" and the "syllogism of the reasoned fact" is ὅτι and διότι, the same terms that Aristotle uses to designate what are now two scientific questions and that these questions seek to know whether there is such a middle term in a syllogism and what it is.

This last question has a special resonance in the Aristotelian corpus. Often, when Aristotle wants to indicate a substance in contrast with the other categories, he refers to the "what is it?" (τὸ τί ἐστι) or, as it is also rendered, the "what it is" (*Metaph.* Z 1, 1028a13–18). He also uses this expression to refer to the substance (or essential nature) of instances of other categories (1028a36–b2). We might wonder whether the "what is it?" question of the *Posterior Analytics* must always refer to a substantial nature or the essence of something in another category. Can it be a less ontologically charged request simply to identify the middle term? There are passages that suggest that this is what Aristotle has in mind. One example in II 11 claims that when we ask why the Persians declared war on the Athenians, we are seeking to identify what the middle term is; it is, the Athenian raid on Sardis, Aristotle proposes (94a36–b8). But, as I said, this is not a scientific syllogism; its terms can be otherwise. In a scientific syllogism, the middle term belongs necessarily to the subject, and this

---

7 Halper 2017, 57–59.

THE METAPHYSICS OF THE SYLLOGISM 47

condition is met canonically when the middle term is the subject's essential nature or, alternatively, the essential nature of the major term. So, in general, the "what is it?" that is sought as the middle term of a scientific syllogism is some essential nature.

These opening chapters of *Posterior Analytics* II are very important for a number of reasons. In book I, the emphasis is on drawing a conclusion from necessary, causal premises. Here in book II, where the syllogism is being used for inquiry, the assumption is that we know the conclusion: it is prior to us. What we are seeking is the cause, which is prior in nature. There is absolutely no notion of pursuing inquiry by syllogistic demonstration.[8] In inquiry the syllogism works in the opposite direction, from conclusion to middle term. The syllogism turns out to be a means of answering the "what is it?" question. It serves to direct our attention toward looking for a term that can serve in the middle, causal position so that there will be a syllogism, and when such a term is discovered, the syllogism provides evidence that this middle term is a cause.

It hardly makes sense to speak of discovering a real cause in the context of contemporary logic because inferences are derived by deductions in a closed system: a number of propositions or predicates are specified, and nothing new is introduced from the outside. In this type of system, it makes no difference whether the deduction proceeds from premises to conclusion or in the opposite direction. They are mathematically equivalent. Aristotle's syllogistic demonstration is not properly called a "deduction" because his system is not closed. The syllogism does not arrive at a conclusion so much as provide inquiry with a direction: it is a way to determine what is needed, as I said. Once we recognize that a middle term is needed to justify a conclusion, it is easier to find it. Once found, we have scientific knowledge of the conclusion by recognizing the relationships of the terms. The lengthy discussion in II 3–10 of whether the definition can be demonstrated by a syllogism is justified because it shows that the terms of the syllogism cannot simply be rearranged so as to demonstrate the essential definition, the definition that answers the "what is it?" question.[9]

---

8   When Owen 1968, 167 famously declares that Aristotle's sciences do not follow the method he set out in the *Posterior Analytics*, he means that Aristotle's sciences are not demonstrative. Likewise, apparently assuming that syllogism could only be useful to inquiry by demonstrating conclusions, Barnes denies that syllogisms play any role in demonstration, and he proposes that II 1–2 "contain ... directions to the pedagogue on how to construct his lessons" (Barnes 1975, 83).

9   Aristotle recognizes multiple senses of definition, as he explains in II 10. For a good summary of them, see Byrne 1997, 162–63. The definition that expresses the essential nature of the subject term is one type of middle term. Another definition arises from ascribing this nature to the subject term; it is this definition that Aristotle argues cannot be demonstrated.

The scientific syllogism is uniquely directional. If the definition could be demonstrated, then it would not be a first principle. A scientific syllogism must begin (ultimately) from what is indemonstrable (I 3, 72b18–25).

What makes the question of demonstrating a definition interesting is that with a purely formal rearrangement, we *can* create a formally valid syllogism in which the essential definition appears in the conclusion. This is, of course, a syllogism of the fact. We would have circularity if the definition could equally well appear in premises or conclusion. This type of circularity is not a problem in a formal deductive system; rather, it is a requirement of the system. Aristotle is arguing that the syllogism cannot demonstrate a definition without giving up the priority of the definition and, thereby, the possibility of knowing something through the definition. It is because we know something when we know its cause and because the definition is the cause that we cannot demonstrate a definition.

Nonetheless, we can use the syllogism as a tool to help to discover the definition, as I said. The syllogism's conclusion is known prior to inquiry. We are seeking to discover and, so, come to know the essential nature through which the conclusion is known. That the conclusion can be demonstrated from some definition counts as evidence that this is the definition of the essential nature, though that essence must still come to be known by *nous* apart from the demonstration.[10] The *Posterior Analytics* says nothing about attaining noetic knowledge of essences, perhaps because each case is different. However, it does propose some techniques for arriving at definitions though here, too, there are no mechanical procedures. We will look at the techniques later. First, we need to consider the inner and outer terms of a scientific syllogism.

Book II's discussion of inquiry makes clear that the middle term is, canonically, the essential definition of some nature, either the minor or major term, as I said. What are the two other terms? As I said earlier, they are a subject and an essential attribute of that subject, an attribute that belongs to the subject in respect of the nature the definition expresses. Inasmuch as an attribute belongs to the subject through some nature, it must be essential to the subject.

Aristotle provides more detail in I 28. He says there that one science treats one genus, and he includes with the genus its "primary constituents," its species (μέρη), and its "essential attributes" (87a38–39). The "primary constituents" must be the essential attributes of which the essential nature of the genus is composed; that is, the first type of essential attribute that Aristotle distinguishes in I 4 (73a34–37). "Essential attributes" here must refer to the I 4's

---

10   In Halper 2017, 71–96, I show how the opening books of the *Physics* lead the reader to a noetic knowledge of nature.

THE METAPHYSICS OF THE SYLLOGISM

49

second type of essential attributes, those whose definitions include the definitions of their subject. Aristotle's justification for including all these in one science is that the indemonstrables are in the same genus as what is demonstrated from them (87b1–4). The indemonstrables are, as we have just seen, the essential definitions that are the causes of what is demonstrated. The latter are, in turn, the essential attributes of the genus as a whole or of one or more of its species. The essential definition is most plausibly the definition of the genus, and the demonstration shows that the essential attributes belong to each instance of the genus in respect of the genus's essential nature. In short, the scientific syllogism demonstrates the essential attributes that belong to a genus in respect of the genus's essential nature. To put it in the Barbara form:

> Everything with this essential nature has attribute X
> <u>Every instance of the genus has this essential nature.</u>
> ∴ Every instance of the genus has attribute X.

Again, this syllogism is valid primarily because the essential nature is the cause of the genus's having the attribute. The genus is X in respect of its essential nature. An important variation is the scientific syllogism that relies on the essential nature of the attribute rather than the nature of the genus. We will see that it is closely connected with the paradigmatic case.

V

So understood, the scientific syllogism meets all the criteria that Aristotle sets out in I 2. The genus itself is often relatively easy to identify by some character. We can presumably discover it through the procedure that Aristotle sketches in II 19 (compare I 18).[11] After repeated observations of dogs, for example, some common feature "takes a stand" and we come to recognize that there are multiple things with this universal feature. In the same way that we come to recognize the genus of dogs, we recognize that instances of this genus bark. The task for inquiry is to determine why dogs bark. The reason should lie in the dog's nature, that is, in what it is to be a dog. In seeking the nature of dog, we seek

---

11 Identifying the genus seems to be what Charles 2000, 24, takes to be "stage 1" of philosophical inquiry. He is right, but I do not think this is Aristotle's point in the opening lines of II 10. If stage 1 is attained through what II 19 describes, as I think it is, then it occurs together with Charles's stage 2, the grasp of the existence of an individual instance of the universal.

something that accounts for the dog's barking. Just what this nature is remains unclear, but we do have a criterion through which to recognize it: the nature must somehow account for dogs barking.

Since the nature of dogs is obscure, we can consider a nature that is better known, our own. Human beings stand upright. What is the reason? We are rational animals. An upright posture enables us to look at the heavens, and their regular motions are objects of knowledge that we can grasp with reason. A condensed version of multiple syllogisms could go like this:

> The motions of the heavenly bodies are easily observed by beings that walk upright.
> What is always the same and sensible are the motions of the heavenly bodies.
> Knowledge arises from sensation and is of what is always the same.
> Rational animals can have knowledge.
> <u>Human beings are rational animals.</u>
> ∴ Human beings are beings that walk upright.

This reasoning process could also be expressed as a series of syllogisms, a sorites. That way each demonstration can be presented with a single middle term and seen to be true. But there are advantages to my presentation. First, it makes clear that the essential nature of human beings is a necessary term for the inference. Second, it makes clear that there are actually a number of "middle terms" between the genus, human being, and the attribute we are interested in demonstrating. The first of these middle terms is the essential nature of the subject.

The essential nature belongs to the genus immediately (I 15, 79a33–38). That is to say, there is nothing that stands between these two terms: if there were, what is between them would be a middle term, it would be more properly the nature of the genus. Hence, the middle term of the syllogism not only mediates the relation between the extreme terms, but it also stands between them in a sequence of attributes. Ideally, the connection between each adjacent term in the sequence is immediate or, as Aristotle says here, "indivisible" (ἀτόμος). If not, one or more additional terms should appear between them until every term in the sequence follows immediately and is followed immediately. The middle term is not merely a position in a syllogism; it is also a position in a sequence of terms or, equivalently, a sequence of attributes.[12]

---

12 See Barnes 1995, 49–50. The connection must be grasped with *nous*. There is no discussion of how we come to grasp it, but this connection is not rooted in sensation, as is the grasp of the universal that Aristotle discusses in II 19.

THE METAPHYSICS OF THE SYLLOGISM 51

Could there be an infinite number of middle terms between a subject and its attribute? If so, the connection between attribute and subject would not be indivisible. Aristotle addresses this question along with the parallel issues of whether there can be an infinite sequence of subjects or of predicates in a lengthy discussion (I 19, 81b–82a8). That all of these infinities are impossible is hardly surprising: since it is impossible to traverse an infinity, were terms infinite in any of these ways there could be no demonstrative knowledge (84a2–4). Still, it is surprising how much attention Aristotle devotes to the question (82a2–84a2). He argues against an infinity of middle terms between any two terms on the ground that, depending on which term one started from, it would imply either an infinity of predicates (that is, of attributes) or an infinity of subjects (I 20). An infinity of attributes of the first type of essential attributes would mean that the subject was unknowable (83b8; 84a25–26). Since there is no attribute of an attribute (83b36–37), a series of attributes of the second type of essential attribute would all be attributes of the subject and their definitions would include the subject along with all the intermediate terms; if a single subject does not admit of an infinite number of attributes of the second type, then there cannot be an infinity of predicates (84a17–25). In arguing against the various kinds of infinities, Aristotle assumes that there are sequences of attributes and that each attribute in the series is immediately connected with what precedes it all the way back to the subject. The assumption is not argued, but Aristotle seems to think that only such sequences could make possible demonstrative knowledge. Inasmuch as there is demonstrative knowledge, there must be such sequences of attributes.

It is, therefore, apparent that in explaining how an infinite sequence of attributes or subjects would undermine demonstrative knowledge, Aristotle is tacitly equating the series of attributes with a demonstrative syllogism or series of syllogisms. If we start from a subject, the first predicate is its essential nature. Then, some essential attribute is predicated of the essential nature. After this, comes another essential attribute, then comes a third essential attribute in the series, and so forth. The first essential attribute is known to belong to the subject through the essential nature. That is the first syllogism. The second essential attribute in the series belongs to the subject through the first essential attribute. That is to say, it can be ascribed to the subject by means of a syllogism that has the first essential attribute as its middle term. Since the first essential attribute belongs to the subject through the essential nature, the second one also belongs to the subject ultimately through the essential nature. A third syllogism ascribes the third essential attribute to the subject through the second essential attribute (as its middle term) and, so, ultimately through the essential nature (see II 18). If this sequence of syllogisms is infinite, then the subject would have an infinite number of attributes, but this is impossible. Again, the assumption here is that *the sequence of attributes is tantamount to the sequence of syllogisms*. This is a sequence of "indivisible" attributes, which is to say that there is no other attribute between any two attributes in the series. This immediacy is, presumably, the key to the possibility of a sequence. Because there is nothing between any two attributes in the series, we grasp their connection immediately. Just as we have a natural human ability to discern that nearness is the cause of non-twinkling, rather than the other way around, we have the ability to recognize that one attribute is immediately connected with another, as is clear from examples.

VI

We have answered our central question: a syllogism exists in a subject as a sequence of immediately connected essential attributes. However, this answer does not really make the syllogism intelligible. An "indivisible" connection links the terms of the syllogism with each other, but it remains unclear whether what the terms refer to are so connected. Do the attributes of a subject genus really constitute a sequence in which each is immediately connected with the next? What about the genus and its attributes would make us think that they do?

We saw earlier that there is a definitional connection between the subject's essential nature and the essential nature of the attributes: one or the other of these is contained in the essential definition of the other. So, the sequence is not a casual collection of attributes; there is an essential connection that is rooted somehow in the natures of the terms, but what is it?

Aristotle talks about arranging essential attributes properly in II 13. The context is his discussion of how to find definitions. He proposes collecting attributes together to define something that, uniquely, has all the characters, but he also suggests reaching a definition by division. In order to be sure nothing is omitted, the division must proceed step-wise and, it seems, include all the preceding differentiae. Not every animal is split-winged or whole-winged, but every winged-animal is. If, then, the genus animal is differentiated by differentiae that together include all animals, each of these differentiae can be further differentiated (96b35–97a8). Getting the right sequence of essential attributes (type 1) is crucial for the definition of the ultimate species, for the split-winged will include winged, as well as its genus, animal (as Aristotle argues in *Metaph.* Z 12). Conversely, while the science of zoology treats the genus of animal and its essential attributes, there is nothing that is simply animal. Every *actual* ani-

THE METAPHYSICS OF THE SYLLOGISM 53

mal is an animal of some sort. That is to say, the genus is necessarily differentiated.

Let me explain. Consider the following sequential reasoning: An animal is a substance that is capable of moving itself. In order to move itself it must have an organ for motion. Organs of motion must propel the animal on land, water, or air. Propelling an animal on land, water, or air requires organs specifically fitted to each of these, that is, legs, fins, or wings, or comparable organs.

What's striking about this particular sequence of attributes is the way each term follows what precedes it. We can say, abstractly, that all animals can move themselves; but no animal can *actually* move itself without organs fitted to the task, and the motion is always accomplished in a characteristic way that is suited to the medium. Thus, the essential nature of a genus-like animal is a kind of potentiality that can only be realized in something actual. The transition between this potentiality and the actual realization occurs through steps, that is, through species, until we arrive at the ultimate differentiae, characters that are sufficiently determinate to have a concrete existence. Again, the nature of an animal, "having the capacity to move," does not cause motion nor does it issue in a specific motion. By referring to wings, legs, and fins, we are indicating particular modes of motion, distinct ways in which species make actual what it is to be an animal. That every animal must have some such organ follows from the nature of an animal. We can easily represent the sequence of thought with a series of syllogisms about the genus, animal. The point is that such syllogisms are possible because of the way that the attributes exist.

We can go further by looking at some of these species. Having wings specifies a mode of motion and, thereby, a species of the genus animal. Wings are of two types, split or whole. The wings of birds are split into feathers that are themselves divided, in contrast with the whole wings of insects (*Parts of Animals* IV 12, 692b12–15). With this last division, we have a definition that is more concrete and, thereby, closer to actual existence. The split-winged species is itself a genus, birds, and it has its own differentiae. Aristotle distinguishes birds whose large wings allow them to hold other animals as they fly, birds whose wings allow them to fly swiftly to escape danger, and birds whose wings are so small relative to their bodies that they cannot fly (693b26–694a7). The size of the wings indicates not just their mode of flight or their absence of flight but important details about their modes of life. These particular kinds of wings serve to allow the potentialities inherent in their genera to be realized. Since the abstract genera exist only in concrete instances, the genus must be differentiated. My claim is that differentiation occurs through a necessary succession of attributes that are immediately connected with each other and the initial genus.

If this interpretation of II 13 is correct, then we can see how a sequence of attributes can be constituted from "indivisible" connections and yet be propelled forward from the most general to the more specific. Since the more specific natures (split-winged animal) include within themselves the more general characters (animal), whatever belongs to animal must also belong to split-winged animals. Thus, we have the basis for one sort of scientific syllogism.

This account will do for the first type of essential attribute. The second type of essential attribute is more important for science. For these, it is the definition of the attribute that includes the definition of its subject. Number's being odd or even is one example; the definitions of odd, for example, includes number. Using the definition of odd as the middle term, we can construct a syllogism whose conclusion is that some numbers are odd. However, this is not a scientific syllogism because odd does not belong to every instance of the genus. A scientific syllogism about number would require treating "odd or even" as a single predicate whose definition is, perhaps, "divisible by 2 or not divisible by 2." The conclusion would be: number is odd or even.

The alternative is to use the essential attribute to delimit a species. Thus, Aristotle suggests that the shedding of leaves is the coagulation of sap at the junction of leaf-stalk and stem (II 17, 99a24–29). Hence, we have the following syllogism:

> The coagulation of sap at the junction of leaf-stalk and stem is the shedding of leaves.
> Vines, figs, and other trees have sap that [in cold temperatures] coagulates at the conjunction of leaf-stalk and stem.
> ∴ Vine, figs, and other trees shed their leaves.

Aristotle's challenge here is to characterize the genus of those trees that shed their leaves. We call such trees "deciduous trees," but if this were the subject of the syllogism, the conclusion would be tantamount to "trees that shed their leaves shed their leaves." Instead, Aristotle looks for what figs, vines, and other such trees have in common. They are all broad-leafed. Perhaps, he thinks that broad leaves, by virtue of their size, require a great deal of sap and, therefore, die when cooler temperatures cause that sap to coagulate at the narrow point where leaf meets stem. If so, then the three terms in the syllogism are indissolubly linked. Thus, we have a kind of sequence here: broad leaves, coagulation of sap, and shedding leaves. Each of these terms is a kind of an abbreviation of something larger: the broad leaves requiring much sap from the trunk to sustain them, the cool weather coagulating the sap at the narrow point where

THE METAPHYSICS OF THE SYLLOGISM   55

leaf stem meets branch, and leaves that are deprived of their nourishment dying and falling off. So understood, each term leads to the next.

There is another more famous example that depends on the definition of the attribute. Why does the moon suffer eclipse?[13] The answer depends on noticing that the moon only suffers eclipse when it is full, and that the moon is only full when it is directly in line with the sun and the earth. In this configuration, the earth is between sun and moon and capable of cutting off the light from the sun and, thereby, casting a shadow on the moon. The syllogism that is most immediately apparent is the syllogism of the fact:

> A full moon that is shadowed without there being anything between it and earth is eclipsed.
> The moon is sometimes, when full, shadowed without there being <u>anything between it and earth.</u>
> ∴ The moon is eclipsed.

On this rendering the full moon's being shadowed is, as the middle term, the cause of its being eclipsed. The syllogism of the reasoned fact results when we have an essential definition of the eclipse in the middle term:

> Sunlight blocked by the interposition of the earth between moon and sun is an eclipse.
> The Moon can be prevented from reflecting the sun's light by the inter<u>position of the earth.</u>
> ∴ The Moon can suffer eclipse

This formulation of the syllogism omits the phase of the moon that is essential for understanding the eclipse. We need another syllogism or other premises:

> The interposition of the earth between the sun and moon in a way that leaves the moon in shadow is an eclipse.

---

13   On this example, see Goldin 1996. The middle term in the syllogism of the fact is usually understood to be the moon's inability to provide enough light for things on earth to cast shadows. As Goldin notes (122n) this is an "artificial" character. Bronstein 2016, 48, also distinguishes two types of syllogisms: those in which the middle term is the essential definition of the subject (his example is the nearness of the non-twinkling planets) and those in which the middle term is the essential definition of the essential attribute (his example is the deciduous tree).

When moon is full, its circuit has brought it to a place where the sun illuminates it from behind the earth, and then the earth can be interposed between moon and sun and leave the moon in shadow.

∴ Hence, the full moon can suffer eclipse.

What I have here expressed as one scientific syllogism could be expressed as multiple syllogisms. What is important to see is that there are series of essential attributes that stand between the moon and the eclipse, the last of which is the essential definition of the eclipse. Taken as a whole, the syllogism constitutes demonstrative knowledge of the eclipse. As is often the case in the *Posterior Analytics*, Aristotle does not fully elaborate all the terms necessary for a syllogism.

So far, I have mentioned three sorts of essential attributes of the second type that can be demonstrated by scientific syllogisms: attributes like "odd or even" that belong collectively to their subjects, attributes like "eclipsed" that do not always belong but must be able to belong to their subjects, and attributes like "the shedding of leaves" that are as closely connected with their subjects as having angles that sum to two right angles is connected with all triangles. In each case, we have seen a sequence of necessarily linked attributes.

Must subjects have attributes? If so, why? Let me suggest that the answer to these questions can be seen from an important argument in the *Metaphysics*. In Z 17 Aristotle asks why the composite of material parts is one substance. He reasons that the materials cannot be made one by some other material because we would, then, have to ask the same sort of question, what is it that makes this material and all the others one? Instead, the cause of unity must be some principle that is not material, a form. It becomes clear by the last chapter of book H that this form is an actuality, which is to say, the materials are one insofar as they are capable of acting together. The practical import of this conclusion is that animals are defined by their *capacity* to move themselves, as we have seen, and human beings by our capacity for thought. The *Metaphysics* is concerned with the unity of each substance; other theoretical sciences have the opposite concern: animals could not move themselves without their having bodies, nor could human thought occur without the sensible images of imagination, images that require organs capable of sensation. In these cases, the essential natures that define subjects *require* attributes because they exist not alone, but in some matter. It is the task of the particular sciences to spell out the relations of these essential natures to the sequences of attributes that they entail. At one point in the *Posterior Analytics*, Aristotle claims that the definition signifies something that is one and the demonstration also signifies something one because "what a man is" differs from man's being (II 7, 92b9–11).

THE METAPHYSICS OF THE SYLLOGISM 57

The unity that the definition signifies is an essential nature, such as the essential nature of human being. The syllogism signifies the unity of an essential nature and the attributes that necessarily belong to it. These attributes are what make the nature a real being; the essence requires them for its real existence. The essence can only exist in some matter that is fitted to it, and from the perspective of the essence, these materials and their characteristics are essential attributes.

Some examples make clear how these attributes are connected with their essences. As I said, in order to think, we need sensation. Sensation, in turn, requires sense organs that can be affected by the elements without being destroyed by them. These organs require other organs that sustain them in such a way that they can fulfill their purpose. Thus, Aristotle supposes that our long and folding intestine helps us to think; for were our intestine not as long as it is, we would be constantly hungry and, therefore, unable to listen to long lectures (*On the Generation of Animals* I 4, 717a21–b4; compare *PA* III 14, 675b22–28 and *Tim.* 73a). Similarly, human beings stand upright in order to see the heavens and, thereby, to be able to realize our capacity to reason about what is eternal. The point is that the material bodily parts are structured so as to help promote the actual functioning that is our human nature (*PA* I 5, 645b14–20; 1, 640a33–b4). These parts and their dispositions are, I suggest, a fourth sort of essential attribute of the second type.

Starting from one of these attributes, we can find a sequence of attributes that extends to an essential nature through which it can be understood. However, it would be hard or impossible for us to start from the essence and derive the attributes.[14] In other words, we can follow a sequence of attributes back to a nature, but we cannot generally start from a nature and derive specific

---

14   Bronstein 2016, 32–35, argues that Aristotle thinks that the "expert scientist" can learn from demonstration on the ground that the expert has made the premises of the scientific syllogism, premises that are more known in nature, also be more known to himself. Hence, he thinks the expert can begin with the premises and derive the conclusion. This procedure looks like beginning with essence and deriving the attributes. However, any attribute that appears in the conclusion must also be present in the premises. So, the demonstration does not derive a new attribute. There may be some demonstrations in which someone who knows an essential nature comes to see that it must also have an attribute he had not observed because of its necessary association with one he had observed, though this is not deriving an attribute from a nature. In any case, the expert usually knows the conclusion because it is prior to us. What he learns from the demonstration is that this conclusion is a consequence of an essential nature. That is to say, learning by demonstration is not usually learning a new conclusion, but learning the demonstration, and this demonstration is itself scientific knowledge, as we have seen.

attributes like upright posture or long intestines. There is, thus, a directionality to our knowledge. If the directionality were in the opposite direction, it would be possible to conceive of the syllogism as deriving conclusions. As it is, though, the syllogism serves, first, to direct us toward finding which, among the terms that we know in advance, is the causal middle term and, then, serves to tie together all these terms by expressing their sequential connections.

For us, the thought process proceeds in syllogisms formed by recognizing the sequence of the attributes. A superior mind could conceivably grasp this sequence all at once, through *nous*. As Augustine was later to say of an entirely different subject: time is the extension of God's mind and exists for him all at once, whereas for us it unfolds bit by bit.[15] So, too, we come to know the world gradually one attribute at a time through syllogisms even though these attributes exist as a unity, all together, all at once within the thing known.

VII

Logic is sometimes thought to exist independently of things and, thereby, independently of metaphysics. It is clear that Aristotle does not agree. Not only is the principle of non-contradiction, upon which all demonstration depends (I 11) a subject for metaphysics (*Metaph.* Γ 3–8), but logic is pervaded by metaphysics, as we have seen. I conclude by mentioning two metaphysical issues with Aristotle's account that, I suggest, remain problematic.

He himself broaches the first of them. After distinguishing the syllogism of the fact from the syllogism of the reasoned fact, Aristotle notes that it often falls to one science to use the results of another (78b34–79a16). His point is that while one science will properly demonstrate a conclusion, a different science merely uses this conclusion without demonstrating it or uses a syllogism of the fact. In some of his examples, there is a metaphysical connection between the two sciences: thus, the results of mathematics bear on nautical astronomy because the navigator is concerned generally with mathematics as it exists in the physical world. However, Aristotle also illustrates multiple sciences treating the same subject by claiming that it belongs to medicine to know *that* circular wounds heal more slowly than wounds of other shapes, though it belongs to mathematics to know *why* this is so. This case apparently relies on medicine's being a *pros hen* science, as claimed in *Metaphysics* Γ (1003b1–4). Its subject matter is not a genus in the strict sense, health in a body, but a more broadly understood (*pros hen*) genus, healthy (1003b11–14). But this move is not always

---

15   *Confessions*, book XI, especially chapters 27–31.

THE METAPHYSICS OF THE SYLLOGISM 59

available, and there is good reason to think that many if not most demonstrations must rely on entities and attributes that belong to other genera. That the sum of the angles of a triangle is two right angles is one of Aristotle's favorite examples of an essential attribute's belonging to a genus. The genus is triangles, and the attribute belongs in respect of the nature of the triangle, but the demonstration also uses facts about parallel lines and the angles formed by lines that traverse them. These latter are not included within the genus triangle.[16] Likewise the demonstration that a triangle inscribed in a semi-circle must be a right triangle relies on attributes of circles, but also on the attributes of triangles. What is its subject genus? Does one science treat one genus in such cases? We might suppose that in these examples the pertinent genus is not triangle or circle, but plane figures, for this is how we now understand the subject matter of geometry. However, this move cannot be applied to the syllogistic structure of demonstration: to demonstrate an essential attribute of triangles, we must begin with a subject genus and the essential nature that defines the genus. That we need to rely on features of parallel lines or circles to demonstrate attributes of triangles indicates the richness of relations between all geometric entities, a richness that does not readily fit into the Aristotelian scheme. The issue here is not about mathematics or about using syllogisms to make mathematical demonstrations but about whether these demonstrations can all be neatly fit into a single genus.

There is another metaphysical issue with Aristotle's account of the syllogism. We saw that the syllogism exists in a mind as an inference and in the thing as a sequence of attributes. We have struggled to understand how these attributes are connected to each other and why attributes must exist in such sequences. By considering different kinds of attributes, I have proposed several different ways of answering these questions. As I understand the *Posterior Analytics*, it sets out a way in which demonstrative knowledge is possible. That we do indeed know some things through their causes seems obvious from Aristotle's examples, especially the mathematical ones. The issue is how this is possible. It is possible, Aristotle seems to be saying, if the attributes exist in sequences because a sequence of attributes is the basis of a demonstration. Since no other configuration of nature allows for the possibility of demonstrative knowledge, the attributes must exist in sequences. Moreover, there are plenty of examples of sequences of attributes that we judge to be "indivisible" in their connection. Knowing *that* there must be such sequences does not really explain how their terms are connected. Yet, there is no further explanation

---

16   Apostle 1981, 84, asks why the attribute can be demonstrated in multiple ways, but not how the principles of its demonstration could fall under the genus of triangles.

of how to understand the connection of the attributes. There could not be, for if there were some relation that held between them, there would be something, another term, between them and thus the connection would not be indivisible. Further, if there were something else between the terms, we would need to ask the same question about it and each of them: what is it that connects this intermediate term with each of the extremes? To avoid regress, we must simply accept the existence of immediate terms. Sometimes the immediate term is an actualization of what precedes it, sometimes it is necessary for the thing's actuality, and sometimes it is merely beneficial for this actuality. We can appreciate why there are various sorts of sequences and what these sequences are, but we cannot really understand what connects the attributes in the sequence because it is not anything over and above the attributes themselves. The attributes are connected by their own natures. The angles of a triangle sum to two right angles because they are angles of a triangle. In the strict sense, there is no way to understand why there are sequences of attributes and, thus, why demonstrative knowledge is possible because there is not, nor can there be, an overall formula for the sequence: the connections of the attributes are content or material connections rather than formal connections. Were there some common form of sequences of attributes, logic would indeed exist as an independent science with its own subject matter, and it could be thoroughly known. Instead, logic lies rooted in nature, and we come to be aware of it by coming to know nature. It is, as Aristotle's editors called it, an *organon*, a tool to help uncover, bit by bit, essential natures and their attributes.

COLLOQUIUM 2

Commentary on Halper

Owen Goldin
Marquette University

Abstract

Edward Halper's "The Metaphysics of the Syllogism" argues that the ontological ground of valid inference is found in the necessity of the predications that constitute the premises of the sort of syllogism central to Aristotle's theory: demonstration. I further support his conclusion on the basis of a consideration of the title and structure of Aristotle's *Analytics*, as well as some recent analysis of Aristotle's modal logic. Halper however suggests that the logical form of inference is a result of how the mind sorts out the elements involved in a complex unity. I suggest that it is not primarily the mind that does this work, but language. What the mind does is primarily to be understood as a reflection of what language does, not vice versa.

Keywords

syllogism – demonstration – logic – language – necessity

In *Posterior Analytics* II 1 Aristotle tells us that every theoretical investigation begins with determining whether the subject matter in question exists; this is followed by investigating what it is. Once we know the "what it is" we can arrive at explanations of why something has certain characteristics (89b25–31). We should expect that this is so in regard to one of Aristotle's own great discoveries: the syllogism. Presumably, if we have an adequate understanding of what a syllogism is, we will be in a position to say something about why it functions as it does. What is it about the essence of a syllogism that is responsible for the fact that true propositions whose terms have a particular formal relationship to one another must entail a third proposition? Halper points out that these are questions that have been rarely, if ever, asked of Aristotle. Surely it would be anachronistic to attribute to Aristotle a "formalist" metalogic, according to which logic is a series of rules for the manipulation of certain symbols, allowing for the generation of certain other symbols.[1] Perhaps students of Aristotle may have assumed that his response to the metalogical question concerning the grounds of the indispensability of these rules for language and thought parallels that of most logicians—ignoring the question. But if this is so, Aristotle is most un-Aristotelian in regard to logic, his own innovation (*Sophistical Refutations* 34 184b1–3).

Halper presumes that Aristotle's account of the syllogism meets Aristotle's own requirements for scientific knowledge. He asks what it is it about the world that grounds what is responsible for how the sequence of related terms which constitute a syllogism is revelatory of how things are. As the mind[2] works through a sequence of true propositions that have a certain formal character in relation to one another, it is led to affirm the truth of a further proposition. Because Aristotle accepts the isomorphism of the conceptual and the real, there must be something about the world that grounds the reliability of such reasoning. What can this be? Aristotle says nothing about logical space, and apart from taking the principle of non-contradiction to be a principle of first philosophy, he says little about the metaphysical basis of logic. However, Aristotle does talk at length about the metaphysical basis for demonstration. Demonstrations presuppose basic kinds, with essences that are responsible for other necessary features that belong to those kinds. Halper argues that this ontological commitment grounds the very validity of demonstrations, those inferences that show how these other features are logically entailed by essences. Other kinds of inferences (somehow) derive their validity from the same source.

Halper supports his view that the primary variety of syllogism is demonstration by appealing to *Posterior Analytics* I 14, which argues that the most scientific syllogism is that which is in first figure, for which the middle term occupies the central position in the sequence of terms. For any sound syllogism, the middle term is the cause of our knowing that the major term is truly predicated of the minor. Within a scientific demonstration (which is what Aristotle calls a syllogism of the reason why, as distinguished from a syllogism of the fact), the middle term does more than play this central role in justification: it expresses the *cause* of the conclusion. So although other syllogisms might be formally valid, it is only in the case of a scientific demonstration that the

---

1 Such a formalist account of the rules of inference has been most famously offered by Carnap 1937, Section 17.

2 As will become clear, I hold that Aristotle's syllogisms are not primarily mental processes but linguistic actions. For the time being, no harm will be done in tracing Halper's account of the workings of syllogisms, considered as mental inferences.

COMMENTARY ON HALPER

formal structure mirrors the metaphysical structure of the subject matter. As Halper writes, "Scientific syllogisms have valid forms, but those forms are valid because of the nature of the terms and their relation to each other."

The root of the validity of demonstration then is to be found in that feature of demonstrative premises that allows them to ground the sort of syllogism that reveals the reason why the conclusion holds. This is what Aristotle calls καθ' αὐτό predication. In such a predication one term is predicated of another κατά (on account of) what that other is. A science is concerned with καθ' αὐτά predications alone (APo. I 22, 75a29–31). A science deals with a kind (whether substantial or nonsubstantial) that has a number of features that are closely linked in such a way that, given one, others are found together with it. Within a demonstration, a path is traced within the kind through its various linked features. It is the metaphysical bonds holding simultaneously among the terms that ground the validity of the syllogism. Hence, Halper argues, it is the nexus of καθ' αὐτά bonds that hold among these features that are responsible for how demonstration, and, by extension, all syllogism reveal how things are.

But just because demonstrative inference must be grounded on how certain attributes are necessarily linked to the essence of a kind, why must we say this of all inference? Halper's case would be strengthened if it can be shown that demonstration is the focal variety of syllogism. I offer two other considerations in support. First, the opening of the *Prior Analytics* identifies the object of his inquiry as "demonstration and demonstrative science," and then says inquiry into demonstration must begin with identifying what a premise, a term, and a syllogism are (*Prior Analytics* I 1,24a10–13). Perhaps Aristotle proceeds in this way because an understanding of syllogistic is a precondition for understanding demonstration. Before one understands the species, one must understand the genus. The analysis with which the *Prior Analytics* is concerned is the analysis into perfect syllogisms. The *Posterior Analytics* simply applies this analysis to syllogisms that meet certain additional criteria, by which we consider them scientific. This was the interpretation offered by Alexander and Philoponus. The commentary on *Posterior Analytics* II attributed to Philoponus in the Berlin edition, of uncertain provenance, gives another, more convincing account. The analysis with which the *Posterior Analytics* (and especially its second book) is concerned is *causal* analysis. If the title "Analytics" is not equivocal for the two works, Aristotle has his eye on causal analysis throughout his account of the syllogism,[3] which is precisely Halper's point.

Halper's thesis also derives some support from recent work on Aristotle's modal logic. Aristotle's account of modal syllogisms has often been regarded as

---

3 On this see Goldin 2009.

hopelessly muddled, as he indicates that a first figure universal syllogism with a necessary major premise has a necessary conclusion, but one with a necessary minor premise does not have a necessary conclusion. Taking the necessity involved here to be either de re or de dicto allows for one of these results, but not both. Patterson, and improving on his innovations, Malink and Vecchio,[4] have made great progress in solving the problem. The gist of this recent work is that the problem of the two Barbaras and other alleged inconsistencies in Aristotle's modal logic are resolved if we take the modal operator of necessity to govern neither the whole proposition (as in de dicto necessity) nor the predicate alone (as in de re necessity) but to qualify the predicative bond itself. Recall that as Aristotle understands them, the sciences deal with predicative bonds that have the distinguishing feature of being καθ' αὐτά. This is a feature of the predications as such, not of the term, and not of the whole propositions that serve as premises. So both demonstrations and syllogisms of necessity concern predications with a special bond of necessity between subject and predicate. This suggests that the syllogisms of necessity discussed in the *Prior Analytics* simply *are* demonstrations, and that the inquiry into the nature of syllogism pursued in the *Prior Analytics* simply is inquiry into the nature of demonstration. (It must however be admitted that it is unclear exactly how the modal syllogistic of the *Prior Analytics* is supposed to be applicable to demonstration. A demonstration has as its conclusion a universal predication "all S is P," where the predication happens to be καθ' αὐτό and necessary; the conclusion is not "all S is-necessarily P," which is the form of the conclusion of a modal Barbara syllogism, as Aristotle understands it.)

Halper's account faces an obvious objection: Aristotle recognizes the validity of syllogisms that are not demonstrative; they could, for example, be dialectical, rhetorical, or practical. In the latter two cases, at any rate, we are dealing with terms that do not have the requisite relations of necessity among one another. Consider the syllogism "all of my socks are in the top drawer; my athletic socks are socks; therefore my athletic socks are in the top drawer." Here there is no tight metaphysical connection between being a pair of socks and being in the top drawer; yet the syllogism is valid. Prof. Halper says that it is the "formal resemblance" between this sort of inference and the syllogism in the strict sense, the demonstration, that ensures its validity. But why is formal resemblance enough to guarantee validity? For there to be formal resemblance, certain formal features must be shared, and it is these formal features

---

4 Patterson 2002, Malink 2013, Vecchio, 2016. Vecchio's main innovation is to show how the use of obversion is both consistent with Aristotelian semantics and metaphysics, and allows for the resolution of some problems remaining on Malink's account.

COMMENTARY ON HALPER
65

(as opposed to other ones) that ensure validity. What is it about these formal features that gives them this epistemological significance? I worry that our problem about the grounds of logical form and how it relates to ontological truth has reemerged.

I propose the following admittedly speculative solution. Recall that syllogism in general is the genus of demonstration. Aristotle understands the genus of a kind as like its matter insofar as the genus has the potentiality for those differentiating characteristics that constitute that kind. This is why the conjunction of genus and differentia expressed in a definition does not signify a duality but a unity; the differentia is not a characteristic over and above the genus, but simply is the genus, considered as determined in a certain way (*Metaphysics* H 6 1045a21–b7). I have elsewhere[5] suggested that this is the way to understand the relationship between syllogism and demonstration, and by extension, the relationship between the kind of (formal) analysis that is the goal of the *Prior Analytics* and the (causal) analysis that is the goal of the *Posterior Analytics*. Syllogism simply is demonstration, considered as indeterminate. And, just as matter can exist without form (though not vice versa), and has certain characteristics by virtue of being the kind of matter it is, so too, there can be syllogism that is not demonstration. And just as matter, properly understood, must be understood as matter for a certain kind of form, so too syllogism in general must be understood as a kind of logos that when fully actualized (that is, when completing its function of making the world intelligible) is demonstration, insofar as it discursively presents the causal connections that hold in the world. This solution is, I think, in the spirit of the innovations and insights that Halper has shared.

I close by considering another aspect of Halper's account of syllogism. Halper points out that the terms of a demonstration refer to attributes that are always found together. They are not separated in either time or in space. It is the mind that distinguishes them in sorting them out by virtue of the order of causal priority. Halper writes:

> For us, the thought process proceeds in syllogisms formed by recognizing the sequence of the attributes. A superior mind could conceivably grasp the sequence all at once, through *nous*. As Augustine was later to say of an entirely different subject: time is the extension of God's mind and exists for him all at once, whereas for us it unfolds bit by bit. So too, we come to know the world gradually one attribute at a time through syllo-

---

5 Goldin 2009.

gisms even though these attributes exist as a unity, all together, all at once within the thing known.

Aristotle however does not limit to a divine mind the simultaneous grasp of all of the terms in a demonstration, and the causal relations that hold among them. At *Posterior Analytics* I 34, we are told that those with the virtue of ἀγχίνοια are said to be able to grasp the middle term of a demonstration in an imperceptible time (ἐν ἀσκέπτῳ χρόνῳ). It is not clear whether Aristotle is saying that all three terms and the relations that they hold to each other are grasped instantly (where ἄσκεπτος means "not involving investigation" (σκέψις)), or that the passage through the syllogism is too quick to notice. The very notion of mental processes occurring so quickly that one is unaware of their passage would pose severe problems for Aristotle, for it would require attributing to him the anachronistic notion of subconscious thought. This puzzle can be avoided if, instead of taking syllogism to be a mental process, we attend to Aristotle's own definition of syllogism, according to which it is a *logos* (APr. I 1, 24b18, *Topics* I 1, 100a25). A *logos* is neither a proposition nor an ordered sequence of propositions—there is no room for "propositions" in Aristotelian ontology. A *logos* is in the category of action,[6] for it is by speaking (*logos*) that one human being communicates with another. To be sure, just as Parmenides insisted that what is for saying is also for thinking (fragments B3, B6.1), and Plato understood διάνοια (discursive thinking) as a kind of inner discourse (*Theaetetus* 189e4–90a7), so for Aristotle too, logos is isomorphic to thought (compare *De Interpretatione* 1 16a3–6). Even if Aristotle does not posit an inner language ("Mentalese") he surely holds that linguistic communication is possible insofar as the structure of what is spoken somehow corresponds to the structure of what is thought.

Nonetheless, I do not think that it is nitpicking to emphasize that discursive speech is primarily linguistic, not mental. Aristotle posits only one kind of mental entity, a νοητόν (an intelligible). But a νοητόν is a monadic form. Aristotle is clear that it is a mistake to say that the νοητόν is a representation of the form in the world: it is the very form that is present in the world.[7] This is what it means to say that the mind is identical with what it knows (*De Anima* III 5 429b26–430a9). Aristotle's account of propositional knowledge is cloaked in obscure metaphor: when one entertains what (we would call) a proposition,

---

6 On the metaphysical importance of this, see Goldin 2002.

7 This is the gist of *Metaphysics* Z 6: a substance (that which is) and the what is it (that which is the object of knowledge) are one and the same. Otherwise, what is known would be a conceptual entity, and not the thing known.

COMMENTARY ON HALPER

this is a matter of the production of a new identity by the faculty of *nous*.[8] A complex such as "the cat is black" is derived from an inner act of unification of the terms "cat" and "black." At 430b26 we are told that the predicative complex (of the form τι κατά τινος) is a φάσις, a kind of inner saying (or, as the Revised Oxford translation would have it, an "assertion"); this linguistic act, with discrete parts, is distinguished from the unity of objects of thought that Aristotle had just been discussing. Thought unifies; it is language that breaks the thought into parts, and then creates new unities: propositions and inferences with parts that can be distinguished according to the causal order of the states of affairs to which they refer. This suggests to me that what Halper is saying about inferential thought—that it breaks into a multiplicity the features of things that, in spite of their sequence of causal priority and posteriority, cohere as a unity in things—should rather be said of inferential discourse.

---

8 Ἡ μὲν οὖν τῶν ἀδιαιρέτων νόησις ἐν τούτοις περὶ ἃ οὐκ ἔστι τὸ ψεῦδος, ἐν οἷς δὲ καὶ τὸ ψεῦδος καὶ τὸ ἀληθές σύνθεσίς τις ἤδη νοημάτων ὥσπερ ἓν ὄντων ἀλλ᾽ οὖν ἔστι γε οὐ μόνον τὸ ψεῦδος ἢ ἀληθὲς ὅτι λευκὸς Κλέων ἐστίν, ἀλλὰ καὶ ὅτι ἦν ἢ ἔσται. τὸ δὲ ἓν ποιοῦν ἕκαστον, τοῦτο ὁ νοῦς. "The thinking of indivisibles is found in those cases where falsehood is impossible: where the alternative of true or false applies, there we always find a sort of combining of objects of thought in a quasi-unity.... However that may be, there is not only the true or false assertion that Cleon is white but also the true or false assertion that he *was* or *will be* white. In each and every case that which unifies is thought" (Revised Oxford Translation), *DA* 43026–8, b4–6. Note the it is *nous* that unifies the νοημάτα; a proposition does not itself subsist as a νόημα.

COLLOQUIUM 2

Halper/Goldin Bibliography

Apostle, H.G., tr. and ed. 1981. *Aristotle's Posterior Analytics*. Grinnell: Peripatetic Press.

Barnes, J. 1975. Aristotle's Theory of Demonstration. In *Articles on Aristotle: 1. Science*, eds. J. Barnes, M. Schofield, and R. Sorabji, 65–87. London: Duckworth.

Barnes, J. 1981. Proof and Syllogism. In *Aristotle on Science. The "Posterior Analytics." Proceedings of the Eighth Symposium Aristotelicum*, ed. E. Berti, 17–59. Padova: Editrice Antenore.

Barnes, J. 1993. *Aristotle's Posterior Analytics*. 2nd ed. Clarendon Aristotle Series. Oxford: Clarendon Press.

Barnes, J, ed. 1995. *The Cambridge Companion to Aristotle*. Cambridge: Cambridge University Press.

Bronstein, D. 2016. *Aristotle on Knowledge and Learning: The* Posterior Analytics. Oxford: Oxford University Press.

Byrne, P.H. 1997. *Analysis and Science in Aristotle*. SUNY Series in Ancient Greek Philosophy. Albany: State University of New York Press.

Carnap, R. 1937. *The Logical Syntax of Language*. New York: Humanities Press.

Charles, D. 2000. *Aristotle on Meaning and Essence*. Oxford Aristotle Studies. Oxford: Clarendon Press.

Goldin, O. 1996. *Explaining an Eclipse: Aristotle's Posterior Analytics 2.1–10*. Ann Arbor: University of Michigan Press.

Goldin, O. 2002. To Tell the Truth: Dissoi Logoi 4 & Aristotle's Response. In *Presocratic Philosophy: Essays in Honour of Alexander Mourelatos*, eds. V. Caston and D. Graham, 232–49. Burlington: Ashgate Press.

Goldin, O. 2009. The Problem of the Title of the *Posterior Analytics*, and Some Thoughts from the Commentators. *Documenti e Studi Sulla Tradizione Filosofica Medievale* 20: 127–47.

Halper, E.C. 2005. *One and Many in Aristotle's* Metaphysics*: The Central Books*. 2nd ed. Las Vegas: Parmenides Press.

Halper, E.C. 2017. "Aristotle's Scientific Method." In *Reading Aristotle: Argument and Exposition*, eds. W. Wians and R. Polansky, 50–96. Leiden: Brill.

Malink, M. 2013. *Aristotle's Modal Syllogistic*. Cambridge: Harvard University Press.

Owen, G.E.L. 1968. Tithenai ta Phainomena. In *Aristotle: A Collection of Critical Essays*, ed., J.M.E. Moravcsik, 167–90. South Bend: University of Notre Dame Press.

Patterson, R. 2002. *Aristotle's Modal Logic: Essence and Entailment in the Organon*. Cambridge: Cambridge University Press.

Priest, G. 2006. *In Contradiction: A Study of the Transconsistent*. Oxford: Clarendon Press.

Vecchio, D. 2016. *Essence and Necessity in the Aristotelian Modal Syllogistic*. PhD diss, Marquette University.

COLLOQUIUM 3

Likely and Necessary: The *Poetics* of Aristotle and the Problem of Literary Leeway

Jean-Marc Narbonne
Université Laval, Québec

Abstract

Taking as a starting point a crucial passage of Aristotle's *Poetics* where poetical technique is declared to be different from all other disciplines in human knowledge (25, 1460b8–15), I try to determine in what sense and up to what point poetry can be seen as an autonomous or *sui generis* creative activity. On this path, I come across the so-called "likely and necessary" rule mentioned many times in Aristotle's essay, which might be seen as a *limitation* of the poet's literary freedom. I then endeavour to show that this rule of *consistency* does not preclude the many means by which the poet can astonish his or her audience, bring them into error, introduce exaggerations and embellishments on the one hand (and viciousness and repulsiveness on the other), have the characters change their conduct along the way, etc. For Aristotle, the poetic art—and artistic activities in general—is concerned not with what *in fact is* or what *should be* (especially ethically), but simply with what *might be*. Accordingly, one can see him as historically the very first theorist fiction, not only because he states that poetry relates freely to the *possible*, but also because he explains why poetry is justified in doing so.

Keywords

poetic – imagination – creativity – fiction – tragedy

I

Before taking up a more technical discussion about the status of that which occurs "according to the likely or the necessary" in the *Poetics* of Aristotle, I would like to ask: what position, epistemologically speaking, does poetics occupy in the edifice of Aristotelian science? Likewise, I wish to determine what

© KONINKLIJKE BRILL NV, LEIDEN, 2018 | DOI 10.1163/22134417-00331P08

70   NARBONNE

types of discourse and knowledge are promoted by poetry, and, by extension, by art itself, in the realm of human existence.

To that end, I will begin with a short statement we find near the end of the *Poetics*. Curiously, this proposition, whose importance is absolutely capital, has not attracted the attention of the commentators as much as we might have expected.[1] The statement concerns what we can call the standard of *correctness* (legitimacy, validity, etc.,) of poetic discourse as such.

> Since a poet represents, just like a painter or some other maker of images, at any moment he is necessarily representing one of three things, either things as they were or are, or things as people say and think [they were or are], or things as they should be. These things are expressed in diction in which there are exotic names, metaphors [*we will come back to these*] and many modifications of diction; we grant these to poets. In addition, there is not the same [standard of] correctness in the art of civic life as in that of poetry (οὐχ ἡ αὐτὴ ὀρθότης ἐστὶν τῆς πολιτικῆς καὶ τῆς ποιητικῆς), nor is there in any other art as in that of poetry (οὐδὲ ἄλλης τέχης καὶ ποιητικῆς).
> (25, 1460b8–15, translation by Richard Janko 1987)

The apparent meaning of this categorical declaration of Aristotle is that poetical discourse arises *neither* from the political (or *civic life*), to which it is often associated (especially in "ethical" or "moralizing" understandings of poetics), *nor* from any other form of art, *technê*—a term referring to the ways each particular art has of *carrying out* that which it knows.

Let us observe that from the beginning of the passage cited, the poet, who is classified by Aristotle alongside the painter or any other *producer of images*, is defined as an *imitator* (εἰκονοποιός). It is essential that this term not be interpreted in a purely restrictive sense. The poet does not simply imitate *that which is or that which was*, but, already with more leeway, that which *seems to be* or *is reported to have existed*, or, with an even greater license, that which *should be*, in other words, that which the poet himself *wishes to see happen*. This is immediately confirmed by what Aristotle writes a little further on in the same chapter: "It may be impossible that there are people like those Zeuxis painted, *but he painted them better* (βέλτιον); for that which serves as a model should *be superior* (ὑπερέχειν)" (25, 1461b12–14). That which serves as an example then

---

1   Halliwell 1998, 3, 24 *sq.*, 132, 335, has shown himself to be the interpreter who is the most sensitive to that "resounding affirmation" (3) and who has drawn the proper conclusion, namely that poetry "should not be subjected to simple and direct evaluation in terms of external criteria—moral, political or otherwise" (4).

THE *POETICS* OF ARISTOTLE AND THE PROBLEM OF LITERARY LEEWAY 71

must be superior, it must trump the *observed* reality. As such, we can observe that the poet or painter enjoys a considerable degree of leeway. His *representation-imitation* arises more from the *transformation* or the *transfiguration* of reality than from simple *passive reproduction* or *passive transposition* of it.[2]

In what way does Zeuxis paint better? From where does he draw his inspiration? From his intellect? From his imagination? Does he paint the figures larger? Make them more muscular? More intense and imposing than in reality? And if so, in what way? Aristotle does not specify here, but it is obvious that he is granting to the poet, as to the painter or sculptor, a real creative leeway. We can see this at the end of the sentence, where he concludes "For these are the things we grant to the poets" (δίδομεν γὰρ ταῦτα τοῖς ποιηταῖς). We concede to poets, painters or sculptors, etc., the right or the possibility to take a certain liberty vis-à-vis the facts themselves, vis-à-vis empirical objectivity, etc. This is the same idea that Aristotle has already announced in chapter 9: "It is also obvious from what we have said that it is the function of a poet to relate not things that have happened, but things that may happen (ἀλλ᾽ οἷα ἂν γένοιτο), that is that are possible in accordance with probability or necessity" (9, 1451a36–38).

Let us then come back to the question of the status of poetry, which is neither political nor technical in the ordinary sense of the term. What we find in that text is a double delimitation that is clearly fundamental. A *poetics* cannot be evaluated in terms of the standard of *correctness* that applies to politics. Likewise, it cannot be judged in the manner of other technics. As such, poetics constitutes a fairly isolated case in the order of knowledge. In the first place, it does not belong to the theoretical sciences (theology, mathematics, physics), taken by Aristotle to be superior to absolutely all other sciences.[3] At the same

---

2   As Halliwell 2002 has stated, "No greater obstacle now stands in the way of a sophisticated understanding of all the varieties of mimeticism, both ancient and modern, than the negative associations that tend to color the still regrettably standard translation of mimesis as 'imitation' ..." (13). It is worth recalling that already in 16th century, Philip Sidney in his *Defence of Poesy* (1580), could render the term *mimesis* by talking of "a representing, counterfeiting, or figuring forth" (Macardle, 1964, 8). In my view, the use of the expression *"figuring forth"* is a very good means to convey the *active-creative* sense naturally implied in Aristotelian's concept of mimesis. I thank Professor Douglas Hedley for bringing to my attention this very important essay.

3   The superiority of theoretical science lies either in its greater exactitude or in the superior dignity of its object, as Aristotle mentions in *Topics*, 8, 1, 157a9–10, as well as at *De anima* I, 1, 402a1–3: "We count knowledge among the fine and honorable things, and suppose that one kind of knowledge [theoretical knowledge obviously] is finer and more honorable than another owing to its precision or because of its having better and more marvelous objects,"

time, it can be slotted neither under the rubric of the practical sciences (ethics and politics), which are directed towards an *outcome* or an *action* (πρᾶξις), nor that of the other poetical sciences, that is, all other artisanal techniques which aim to produce an artifact, a *work* of some type (ἔργον).

This exceptional status granted to *poetry* in the *Poetics* does not, for all that, come into play in all the other writings where Aristotle gives a general treatment of different productive activities. I will take as an example the famous passage from the *Nicomachean Ethics* VI, 4, which concerns arts or techniques.

> That which may or may not be can be an object produced as well as an object of action. Now *production* is distinct from *action*..., and so practical dispositions with reason are distinct from productive dispositions with reason; and in view of this, the two exclude each other, for no action is a production, and no production is an action.... Every art (τέχνη) is concerned with bringing something into existence, and to think by art is to investigate how to generate something which may or may not exist and of which the [moving] principle is in the producer and not in the thing produced.... (VI, 4, 1140a1–14, trans. H.G. Apostle 1974)

Whereas *acting* is an immanent activity, which remains within itself, as when I practice abstinence or engage in a political action, *production*, for its part, always culminates in a given work, which is both distinct from the agent and is for the sake of itself, as when the architect produces a house. This is why Aristotle emphasizes that the two things are not coextensive (VI, 4, 1140a5).

That *action* and *production* do not include each other does not however preclude the fact that, from another point of view, there exists a possible prerogative of the one over and above the other. To be sure, the two types of activity are distinct from each other, yet they are not simply parallel but rather hierarchical: practical action prevails, in terms of its virtue, over production. As such, Aristotle writes: "This [practical thought] rules productive thought also; for he who produces does so for the sake of something, though a product is not an end without qualification but is relative to something else and is a determinate thing. But an object of action [is an end without qualification] for a good action is [such] an end, and this is what we desire" (modifying Apostle's translation). Aristotle's idea here is that, since the pursuit of happiness is at the base of all human action, all of the objectives of production that the individual

---

modification of the Christopher Shields 2016 translation (I have replaced "cognition" with "knowledge" as a translation of τὴν εἴδησιν). On the Aristotelian division of the sciences, see also the classical passage *Metaphysics* E.1.

THE *POETICS* OF ARISTOTLE AND THE PROBLEM OF LITERARY LEEWAY 73

seeks will be goals that are relative to the ultimate quest that is directly implied by pure and simple action, insofar as it is virtuous. On the other hand, the goal of the architect is not simply to produce a house for the sake of the enjoyment of building a house, but rather for the sake of guaranteeing a way of living well. This living well is in turn the direct and immediate object of acting virtuously, which is the aim of ethics and politics.

In the Aristotelian hierarchy of the sciences then, the (standard) *poiêsis* is positioned on the last level of activities. It is subordinated to the practical sciences, which are themselves supposedly subordinated to the theoretical sciences. As such, the exception which the *Poetics* grants to *poetry*—and by extension to "artistic" art in general[4]—will substantially modify this traditional classification. In what way? Up to what point? It is in a way absolutely impossible to say, for the pure and simple reason that it is only the *Poetics* that attests to the exceptional character of poetry itself. When he speaks of art in other parts of his corpus, he never mentions the peculiar status of poetry. Furthermore, the text itself of the *Poetics* never tells us to which other discipline or to which other domain of knowledge poetry actually belongs. This absence of affiliation with any other theoretical domain, as Donini noted,[5] is a unique feature of the *Poetics*. When we read the *Meteorology* (338a20–27) or *Parts of Animals* (639a12), we know that they belong to the study of physics. The situation is the same in the case of *Nicomachean Ethics* (1094a1, b 11) and the *Rhetoric*[6] (1356a25–27), which concern politics.

For the *Poetics* though, we are not provided with the slightest hint. To be sure, throughout the *Poetics*, Aristotle does discuss topics that are also covered in the other treatises. He brings up, among other things, the problem of passion, language, imitation, choice (προαίρεσις) and of course, of *catharsis*, which

---

4 To be sure, the Greeks did not know "our" system of the fine arts (which include practically speaking poetry, sculpture, architecture and music). They did possess however an authentic system of the arts (contrary to the judgment of Kristeller 1951, 506). At the beginning of the *Poetics*, Aristotle brings together what he calls the arts of imitation: poetry, painting, music, song and dance (1, 1447a18 sq.), to which sculpture obviously belongs as well (25, 1460b8–9). Prior to Aristotle, Plato had already proposed grouping together painting and music (*Statesman* 288c) as the arts of entertainment (παίγνιον), i.e., mimetic arts whose sole aim consists in pleasure and ornamentation. Poetry obviously belongs to this category as well (*Republic* X 601a-b).

5 Donini 2003 rightly emphasizes the exceptional case of this text, for which, contrary to other treatises of Aristotle, we find "no explicit, non-equivocal indication that it belongs to a more general philosophical discipline" (436).

6 The reference to the text of the *Rhetoric* is crucial here, insofar as that discipline is uncontestably the one that shows itself to be closest to the *Poetics*.

he also deals with in the treatment of music at the end of the *Politics*. Nevertheless, despite numerous overlaps, it is impossible to deny: 1) that the *Poetics* itself does not explicitly recognize any epistemological dependence of any sort, and 2) that, on the contrary, the *Poetics* expressly claims for itself a clear autonomy of its mode of expression: a poetics is authorized to approach things in its own fashion. It is in no way *naturalist* in its intention; nor is it in itself ethical or political, even if it does indirectly evoke situations or dilemmas that comprise an ethical-political resonance.[7] The bottom line is that the aim of the poetics is not essentially *prescriptive* but *descriptive*. Its purpose is to paint a portrait of a potentially infinite number of alternative combinations of events, which will be more or less gripping or evocative.

Moreover, we have known for a long time that the background of this discussion about poetic ὀρθότης is the accusation brought up by Plato against poetry in the *Republic*, as well as in the *Laws* (II, 667b7–670b4; 700e). In book X of the *Republic*, Plato attempts in effect to show that the imitator has no knowledge of the arts that he speaks of. The poets, he argues, speaks about war, without knowing anything about military strategy. Has there ever been one poet, asks Plato, who has ever helped us win a war? The poet, from this perspective, is a charlatan who mystifies the public. The saddle is known either by the one who makes the saddle, that is the saddler, or by the one who uses it, the rider. The painter and the poet however do not know anything of value about it. Only the maker of the real thing or the user of the thing possess a veritable knowledge of the thing that is produced. Plato's conclusion is thus unambiguous: "Consequently, the imitator will have neither knowledge or the correct opinion (ὄρθα) concerning the objects he imitates" (X, 602a7). He thus concludes the argument by saying: "imitation is only a banter unworthy for serious people" (X, 60b6–7).

---

7   I would thus keep my distance from an interpretation such as that of Donini for example, who, in attempting to inscribe poetics within political philosophy, does not see how "having emerged from the academy of Plato" Aristotle could have, as we do, conceived "politics and poetics as two profoundly different and (fortunately!) fully autonomous intellectual activities" (Donini 2003, 438). Cf. also 439, where Donini speaks of a "strict continuity between the *Poetics* and *Statesman* VII". Yet the entire debate that Aristotle initiates around the question of *correctness* (ὀρθότης) is instigated, it seems to me, in order to demonstrate that it is necessary to *break out of the Platonic orbit*, with its misappreciation of art and of the entire domain of the fictional as such, which, as we know, can in no way be reduced to simple falsehood. As far as I know, Donini nowhere takes into account the passage at 25, 1460b13–15, of which Lucas 1968 says: "The independence of poetic ὀρθότης suggests the existence of a set of purely aesthetic values."

THE *POETICS* OF ARISTOTLE AND THE PROBLEM OF LITERARY LEEWAY   75

Reacting against this attack on art, Aristotle carries out what we could call a *shift of perspective*: poetic correctness is not of the same nature as scientific or technical correctness; it occurs in a different register or in another sphere. Aristotle immediately provides a concrete example of what he means by this:

> First some [criticisms should be solved] with reference to the art itself. [If] impossibilities have been produced, there is an error; but it is correct, if it attains the end of the art itself. The end has been stated [that is, already] if in this way it makes either that part [of the poem], or another part, more astonishing. An example is the pursuit of Hector." (25, 1460b23–27)

Aristotle's example here is the famous scene from the *Iliad*, in which Hector is pursued by Achilles in front of the walls of the besieged Troy. All the soldiers, immobilized by a simple nod from Achilles, watch quietly the surrealist spectacle of that chase. Aristotle has already mentioned shortly beforehand in chapter 24 this same episode:

> [The poet] should put what is amazing (θαυμαστόν) into his tragedies but the epic admits with much more ease the irrational (τὸ ἄλογον), from which amazement arises most, because [the audience] does not see the person in action. For the passage about the pursuit of Hector would obviously be laughable on the stage, with the Greeks standing still and not pursuing him, and Achilles forbidding them to do so, but it passes unnoticed in the epic verses. (24, 1460a10–17)

Aristotle's intention here is to show that the improbable nature of the scene described by Homer matters little in comparison with the effective way that Homer deploys in that scene. Essentially, Homer exposes us to the appalling catastrophe of the fall of Troy through the sudden panic of Hector.

II

Granting then that the poet must be accorded a great deal of liberty, I want to now look at the problem posed by the rule, which Aristotle often comes back to, of "what happens likely and necessarily" for this literary license. First, let us recall that we can count 10 total occurrences of this pair of terms: 7, 1451a12–13; 8, 1451a28; 9, 1451a37; b9 and 35; 10, 1452a20; 11, 1452a24; 15, 1454a34, 35–36 and 36. Second, that the εἰκὸς / ἀναγκαῖον formula is nowhere to be found outside the *Poetics*, which is in itself a very significant point. It is not even to be found in the *Rhetoric*,[8] which demonstrates just how much the *Poetics* is independent of all other texts in the Aristotelian corpus. Third, that we must come to understand how the term "necessary" (one of the two components of the likely/necessary pair) carries a meaning here that is mainly metaphoric. This entails that there is *stricto sensu* no causal necessitation between the components of the narrative. I know that Aristotle sometimes claims apparently the opposite, but he does so to express an ideal, to indicate that the parts of the plot must be well connected and constitute a sort of whole,[9] recognizing himself that this so-called necessity is not always present, as in episodic stories (9, 1451b34–35). He acknowledges himself that the poet can engender surprises, astonishments, unexpected events, that he may exaggerate the qualities and the defects of his characters, etc. (24, 1460a17–18; 25, 1460b23–27; 1461a9–15; 1460b32–35), declaring even that "a believable impossibility is preferable to an unbelievable possibility" (1461b11–12), that impossibilities are correct if they "attain the end of art as such" (1460b24–25). Moreover, Aristotle sometimes forgets to mention 'necessity' in his description of likely events (1451b11–15; 1451b29–32; 1455a17–19),[10] so much so that the *muthos* is elastic enough to

---

8   The only apparent parallel that could be found occurs at *Rhetoric* II 1420b27–28: "to refute a conclusion as improbable is not the same thing as to refute it as not necessary (ἔστι δὲ οὐ ταὐτὸ λῦσαι ἢ ὅτι οὐκ εἰκὸς ἢ ὅτι οὐκ ἀναγκαῖον)" (Translation Rhys Roberts 1984 modified). Yet this passage does not represent a true parallel, since it is not there to emphasize the unity, be it likely or necessary, of the events that comprise the plot, that is to say the *muthos*. Obviously, the passage at 1402b29–30 (ἀεὶ εἰκός, ἀεὶ καὶ ἀναγκαῖον), represents even less of a parallel.

9   In the same sense, Halliwell 1987 notes: "It is curious that Ar. should repeatedly mention necessity in the *Poetics*, since he elsewhere states that few things in the human world can be seen as truly necessary. I take the essential point to be that Ar. wishes the links in a plot-structure to be as causally tight as possible, and the reference to necessity stresses this. Indeed, human actions are not necessary but of the type that can be, not be, and also be otherwise (*Eudemian Ethics* 1224a4 sq.; *Nicomachean Ethics* 1139b7–9; *Rhetoric* 1357a25; 1368b33–36, etc.)" (100n2).

10   A point nicely argued by Armstrong 1998, 447–455. This can be seen as a flaw in D. Frede's analysis when she writes: "the fact that he continues to pair off *necessity* and 'likeness' together throughout the *Poetics*, while there is no such combination in the *Rhetoric*, suggests that the terminological change in the *Poetics* is not one of softening the conditions ..." (209). On the other hand, I do agree with Frede 1992 that Aristotle has the contradictory "twofold task of combining the unusual and the likely" (209). The same mistake is to be found in Riu 2011, who says that "always, when he speaks of the construction of history [in the *Poetics*] Aristotle mentions necessity" (183, cf. 201), while admitting later on that in comedy's construction of the *muthos* (51b12–13), Aristotle "does not speak of necessity" (203).

THE *POETICS* OF ARISTOTLE AND THE PROBLEM OF LITERARY LEEWAY

77

permit a measure of leeway in its structure. Fourth, that one must realize that the concept of the *likely*, the *expected* (τὸ εἰκὸς), can in no manner be directly linked up with the concept of the ὡς ἐπὶ τὸ πολύ, "the most frequent." One must remember that this latter, statistical concept is extremely fecund in the whole of Aristotle's oeuvre (approximately 262 occurrences throughout the corpus), particularly in his ethics. But he uses that expression only one time in the *Poetics* (making it a curious hapax), in fact early in chapter 7 (1450b26–34),[11] and he purposively *avoids using it* in the rest of the treatise.[12] This state of affairs leads us to think that the poetic εἰκὸς must be distinguished from what Aristotle otherwise takes to be the general notion of εἰκὸς. The necessity of this distinction follows from the well-known fact that the 'likely' is often elsewhere connected with the 'most frequent' in Aristotle's corpus, for instance in the *First Analytics* (II, 70a4 and following),[13] and especially in the *Rhetoric* (I, 1357a34; II, 1402b21), a text that is usually seen in close relation to the *Poetics*.[14] My objection here is as follows: if in one way or another, one keeps the εἰκὸς in strict line with the ὡς ἐπὶ τὸ πολύ—contradicting Aristotle's cautious avoidance, which cannot be

---

11   *Poetics* 7, 1450b26–34: "A whole is that which has a beginning, a middle and a conclusion. A beginning is that which itself does not necessarily follow something else, but after which there naturally is, or comes into being, something else. A conclusion, conversely, is that which itself naturally follows something else, either of necessity or for the most part, but has nothing else after it. A middle is that which itself naturally follows something else, and has something else after it. Well-constructed plots, then, should neither begin from a random point nor conclude at a random point, but should use the elements we have mentioned (ὅλον δέ ἐστιν τὸ ἔχον ἀρχὴν καὶ μέσον καὶ τελευτήν. ἀρχὴ δέ ἐστιν ὃ αὐτὸ μὲν μὴ ἐξ ἀνάγκης μετ' ἄλλο ἐστίν, μετ' ἐκεῖνο δ' ἕτερον πέφυκεν εἶναι ἢ γίνεσθαι· τελευτὴ δὲ τοὐναντίον ὃ αὐτὸ μὲν μετ' ἄλλο πέφυκεν εἶναι ἢ ἐξ ἀνάγκης ἢ ὡς ἐπὶ τὸ πολύ, μετὰ δὲ τοῦτο ἄλλο οὐδέν, μέσον δὲ ὃ καὶ αὐτὸ μετ' ἄλλο καὶ μετ' ἐκεῖνο ἕτερον. δεῖ ἄρα τοὺς συνεστῶτας εὖ μύθους μήθ' ὁπόθεν ἔτυχεν ἄρχεσθαι μήθ' ὅπου ἔτυχε τελευτᾶν, ἀλλὰ κεχρῆσθαι ταῖς εἰρημέναις ἰδέαις)" (R. Janko's translation).

12   In this one isolated passage, Aristotle seeks to provide a general characterization of what constitutes a whole, including beginning, middle and end, the idea being that an author must take these general parameters into account in the construction of a narrative. Yet, when it becomes a matter of describing the whole that is specific to poetics, the expression ὡς ἐπὶ τὸ πολύ definitively disappears. For more on this, see A. Schmitt 2011, 362, "Aristotle gives a very formal determination of what beginning, middle and end are .... The fact is that this logical determination holds for every type of whole."

13   "... what men know to happen or not to happen, to be or not to be, for the most part (ὡς ἐπὶ τὸ πολύ) thus and thus, this is probable."

14   It is on this basis that Dupont-Roc/Lallot, 1980, 212 makes reference to the "the objective angle of statistical reality," to which correspond both the *eikos* and the "subjective angle of expectation."

78 NARBONNE

accidental, of the expression later in the treatise—and in strict line with the
necessity factor, as it is standardly interpreted, then everything in the *Poetics*
that is at odds with this rigid scheme would be simply incomprehensible. Secondly, the idiosyncrasy of the poetic realm vis-a-vis the natural and ethical-
political realms would also simply vanish. In other words, one must undo the
strength of the *eikos*-nod and admit, following Aristotle's own invitation, that
"it is probable that many things will happen even against probability (εἰκὸς γὰρ
γίνεσθαι πολλὰ καὶ παρὰ τὸ εἰκός),"[15] a fact that is especially true in the poetic
realm, where the aim, as we know, is to induce "the tragic emotion and the
humane feeling" (1456a21).

III

In order to indicate the sort of literary leeway the poet disposes of according to
Aristotle, I would like to analyse in more detail one particular passage related
to this topic. At 15, 1454a33–36, Aristotle tells us that the pair of terms *likely/
necessary* applies not merely to events but also to characters:

> In the characters too, exactly as in the structure of the events, [the poet]
> ought always to seek what is either necessary or likely, so that it is either
> necessary or likely that a person of such-and-such a sort say or do things
> of the same sort, and it is either necessary or likely that this [incident]
> happen after that one (χρὴ δὲ καὶ ἐν τοῖς ἤθεσιν ὁμοίως ὥσπερ καὶ ἐν τῇ τῶν
> πραγμάτων συστάσει ἀεὶ ζητεῖν ἢ τὸ ἀναγκαῖον ἢ τὸ εἰκός (34) ὥστε τὸν
> τοιοῦτον τὰ τοιαῦτα λέγειν ἢ πράττειν ἢ ἀναγκαῖον ἢ εἰκός (35–36) καὶ τοῦτο
> μετὰ τοῦτο γίνεσθαι ἢ ἀναγκαῖον ἢ εἰκός (36)).

This passage appears at first sight to represent a threat or a counter-argument
to my own thesis, since Aristotle here links together two sorts of constraints:
the likely/necessary constraint applying to events themselves, and the likely/
necessary constraint linked to the characters that are acting. Where is the leeway in all that? The fact is that this leeway exists, both theoretically for Aristotle and practically in the tragedies themselves. We can find it in an important
development in chapter 6 where we read, following the listing of the six parts
of tragedy (spectacle, character, plot, diction, song and reasoning):

---

15 *Poetics* 1456a24–25. I follow here Janko's translation (Barnes is too loose here: "the probability of even improbabilities coming to pass"). Halliwell has also a good rendering: "probability allows for the occurrence of many improbabilities."

THE *POETICS* OF ARISTOTLE AND THE PROBLEM OF LITERARY LEEWAY

The most important of these is the arrangement of the incidents, for tragedy is not a representation of men but of a piece of action, of life, of happiness and unhappiness, which come under the head of action, and the end aimed at is the representation not of qualities of character but of some action; and while character makes men what they are, it is their actions and experiences that make them happy or the opposite. **They do not therefore act to represent character, but the character is included for the sake of the action**[16] (μέγιστον δὲ τούτων ἐστὶν ἡ τῶν πραγμάτων σύστασις. ἡ γὰρ τραγῳδία μίμησίς ἐστιν οὐκ ἀνθρώπων ἀλλὰ πράξεων καὶ βίου [καὶ εὐδαιμονία καὶ κακοδαιμονία ἐν πράξει ἐστίν, καὶ τὸ τέλος πρᾶξίς τις ἐστίν, οὐ ποιότης· εἰσὶν δὲ κατὰ μὲν τὰ ἤθη ποιοί τινες, κατὰ δὲ τὰς πράξεις εὐδαίμονες ἢ τοὐναντίον]; οὔκουν ὅπως τὰ ἤθη μιμήσωνται πράττουσιν, ἀλλὰ τὰ ἤθη συμπεριλαμβάνουσιν διὰ τὰς πράξεις). (6, 1450a15–22)

The translations of this passage, though by no means in itself erroneous, do not seem to me to bring out adequately the truly active sense of πρᾶξις in what Aristotle is saying here. To begin with, the "διά" of "διὰ τὰς πράξεις" is sometimes interpreted as an accusative of interest (*with a view to* = ἕνεκα). Of course, this is grammatically a possible reading, but the accusative of interest is much less frequent than the causal accusative. Halliwell, Janko and Barnes all translate "for the sake of," even though we would expect "through" in the causal sense: "**But their characters are included through their actions.**" Hence, in French, Hardy translates as "ils reçoivent leur caractère par surcroît et *en raison de leurs actions*"; Dupont-Roc/Lallot as "c'est *au travers* de leurs actions que se dessinent leurs caractères," and Gernez as "ils reçoivent leur caractère en même temps *et dans la mesure* où ils agissent." Likewise, A. Schmitt in German translates: "man umfasst die Charaktere *durch die* Handlungen mit" and in Italian we find: "si includono i caratteri in ragione delle azioni."

The central idea here is that, in effect, actions remold or partially modify an initial character, rather than it being the character that, as a preset component, would determine the narrative from the outset. This confirms the previous assertion that the most important thing in tragedy is the composition of the actions (ἡ τῶν πραγμάτων σύστασις, 1450a15), and that without this composition, there would exist no tragedy, even though there could be tragedy without different character types (ἄνευ μὲν πράξεως οὐκ ἂν γένοιτο τραγῳδία, ἄνευ δὲ ἠθῶν γένοιτ' ἄν [1450a23–25]).[17] In other words, character could be *for the sake* of the

---

16   The translation here, supplied by the TLG (*Thesaurus Linguae Graecae*), is W.H. Fyfe 1932.

17   It is obvious that a tragedy *without characters* would literally be impossible, cf. 1450b10–11. Cf. Armstrong 1998, 454n33.

action without being modified *through* the action. But I suggest Aristotle has the second phenomenon in mind, not the first, and I translate accordingly.

Let me now turn to the verb employed in this context, συμπεριλαμβάνουσιν, which is relatively rare in Aristotle (6 total occurrences) and whose sense is difficult to reconstitute. It is clear that "include" is not a sufficiently robust translation. I would prefer something like "gather together" or "include together" (in German "mitumfassen"), which would give: "through their actions they include [gather] together their characters." Interestingly, the Syrian-Arabic reading of the text is συμπαραλαμβάνουσιν,[18] which really means *take along with*.[19] As such, it is necessary to conserve the two components of the combination, recognizing however the priority of the one over the other. Hence, the idea is not that action alone *makes character*,[20] nor that character, as an immobile component, is simply there to serve the action. Rather, in its concrete progression, action makes something new out of the initial character, transforms it and imparts to it an unanticipated dimension.

> Furthermore, if a poet strings together **speeches to illustrate character**, well composed in style and thought, he will not achieve the stated aim of tragedy. Much more effective will be a play with a plot, that is a combination of events, even if it less efficient in these (ἔτι ἐάν τις ἐφεξῆς θῇ ῥήσεις ἠθικὰς καὶ λέξει καὶ διανοίᾳ εὖ πεποιημένας, οὐ ποιήσει ὃ ἦν τῆς τραγῳδίας ἔργον, ἀλλὰ πολὺ μᾶλλον ἡ καταδεεστέροις τούτοις κεχρημένη τραγῳδία, ἔχουσα δὲ μῦθον καὶ σύστασιν πραγμάτων). (1450a29–33)[21]

What is the meaning of this opposition? It implies that you cannot derive a story or a plot simply from the character types involved in it,[22] even if they are well expressed, due to the fact that from definite characters you will only get definite patterns of action, whereas "tragedy is a representation, not of human beings [*that is*, some definite characters], but of action and life (ἡ γὰρ τραγῳδία

---

18 Cf. Tarán/Gutas 2012, 174.

19 By translating "ils reçoivent leurs caractères *par surcroît* ('*as a surplus*')," Hardy is essentially closer to that reading than to the other one.

20 In that sense "ils reçoivent leurs caractères" (Hardy, Genez) is not any more correct, because the figures of a tragedy are not simply empty outlines at the beginning of a piece of theater.

21 My adaptation of Halliwell's translation; "in these" is a rendering of τούτοις, which refer to ῥήσεις ἠθικὰς καὶ λέξει καὶ διανοίᾳ εὖ πεποιημένας.

22 Compare M. Heath 1991, 391: "the outcome of tragic action will not be explicable solely in terms of the character of any single agent."

THE *POETICS* OF ARISTOTLE AND THE PROBLEM OF LITERARY LEEWAY 81

μίμησίς ἐστιν οὐκ ἀνθρώπων ἀλλὰ πράξεων καὶ βίου)" (1450 a 16–17). This is why, says Aristotle, "the aim is a sort of action, not a quality (τὸ τέλος πρᾶξίς τις ἐστίν, οὐ ποιότης)" (1450a18–19), knowing very well that "people are of a certain quality according to their characters (εἰσὶν δὲ κατὰ μὲν τὰ ἤθη ποιοί τινες)" (1450a19). Therefore, ethics can conform to what is expected from characters, but poetics cannot; in other words, the ethical *spoudaios* and the poetical *spoudaios* are not the same and must be distinguished.[23]

Here again the translation of the passage is revealing, because the ῥήσεις ἠθικὰς are not simply "the speeches full of character" (Janko) or "characteristic speeches" (Barnes), expressed in an abstract way, but speeches of some concrete and actual (although fictional) individual and thus "speeches to illustrate [the] character" of this or that particular individual. It is not from this individual character, even well expressed, that the purpose of poetry can be attained. In fact, from individual character, the purpose of poetry will be unavoidably missed, since poetry cannot be reduced to the expression of any specific character.

Accordingly, in the course of events imagined or constructed by the poet, the individual characters with their initial specificity are themselves challenged and forced to adapt themselves to the situation as it inexorably evolves. This is revealed for example in Sophocles' *Ajax*, where the hero proclaims:

> All things the long and countless years first draw from darkness, and then bury from light; and there is nothing which man should not expect: *the dread power of oath is conquered, as is unyielding will.* For even I, who used to be so tremendously strong—yes, like tempered iron—felt my tongue's sharp edge emasculated by this woman's words, and I feel the pity of leaving her a widow and the boy an orphan among my enemies.[24]

The interplay of both these elements makes it possible to imagine all sorts of reversals and setbacks in the life of the protagonists, some less, some more remote from expectations. The crucial power of the objective context in this process is stressed again later in the treatise: "one must consider not only what was said or done..., but also the person saying or doing it, to whom, at what time, by what means and to what end...." (1461 a 5–8).

---

23   On this, see also Riu 2011, 202 and S. Gastaldi 1987.

24   Sophocles, *Ajax*, 646–653 (Jebb's translation). Compare *Antigone*, 563–564: ISMENE: "Yes, Creon. Whatever amount of reason nature may have given them does not remain with those in dire straits, but goes astray." On this phenomenon of change in character, see de Romilly 1968, 88 *sq.*

82 NARBONNE

To come back then to the starting object of our enquiry, we can say that, in the theoretical elaboration Aristotle provides of what it is to be a character in poetical construction, there is already room enough to admit fluctuations and deviations among the so-called *probable/necessary* scheme of reasoning.

IV

Poetical portraits can deviate largely from normal behaviour since the poetic environment is in no way normal itself. Of course, Aristotle is not Lewis Carroll and he would not welcome someone overlaying bizarreness with bizarreness. He does acknowledge though that poetic discourse involves uncommon persons or states of affairs: "for men admire what is remote, and that which is astonishing is pleasant. In poetry, many things conduce to this, and there it is appropriate; for the subjects and persons spoken of are more *out of common*" (*Rhetoric* III, 1404b11–14). Astonishment is pleasant. This is exactly what Aristotle repeats in the *Poetics* after having recalled Hector's story (to which I shall come back in a moment): "What is amazing is pleasant. A sign of this is that everyone narrates [stories] with additions, so as to please" (1460a17–18). To put it bluntly, when telling a story, everyone is lying, but that for a good reason: to please. Now, to please is one of the prominent parameters of any poetical enterprise.[25] So when you overstate and embellish (basically *lie*), you are technically wrong but poetically right.

Let us stop for a moment with the example of Hector, this brave man among the brave, suddenly terrified and fleeing from the pursuing Achilles (XXII, 158). According to Aristotle, the whole scene is unbelievable and yet efficient, efficient *qua* impossible, because it is more striking (ἐκπληκτικώτερον, 1460 b 25). He writes:

> The poet should put what is amazing into his tragedies; but what is irrational, from which amazement arises most, is more admissible in epic because [the audience] does not see the person in action. For the passage about the pursuit of Hector would obviously be laughable on the stage, with the Greeks standing still and not pursuing him, and Achilles forbidding them to do so, but it passes unnoticed in the epic verses. (1460 a 10–16, trans. Janko)

---

25   Cf. e.g., 14, 1453b10–14; 26, 1462a14–17; b11–15.

THE *POETICS* OF ARISTOTLE AND THE PROBLEM OF LITERARY LEEWAY   83

So, this scene is an extravagant and military burlesque, but at the same time a poetically defensible one. Of course, the idea of all the soldiers stopping on Achilles' nod is bizarre, but if you want to represent the tragic destiny of Troy and the unjust collapse of its entire civilization, this extreme portrayal remains appropriate. With the same purpose in mind, when Shakespeare talks in *Romeo and Juliet* about a poison that would simulate death perfectly for no less than 42 hours (the coldness, the breathlessness of it and so on),[26] what he describes is technically impossible but appropriate to the ultimate test of love he seeks to conduct. That is to say, the realm of fiction has its *sui generis* rightness (ὀρθότης), and that is precisely what Aristotle was historically the first to recognize and to authorize, once and for all, in literary theory.

But there is another aspect of this tragic flight from reality I would like to comment on, one which passed unnoticed in Aristotle's analysis: the fact that this indisputable hero, Hector, the commander in chief of the Trojan army, undergoes a significant transmutation in the process of this terrible war. What happened to his former pride and virtue, knowing that virtue is a disposition of character that does not in principle vanish easily?[27] It is neither *necessary nor probable* that such a hero would unrecognizably react cowardly: but then again, the dramatic effect of this literary *descente aux enfers* of Hector is maybe understandable, when one considers the tragic destiny not only of Hector himself but of his entire people, which we see well-reflected later on in *The Persians* of Aeschylus or *The Trojan Women* of Euripides.

---

26   *Romeo and Juliet*, Act IV, scene 1, 92–109: FRIAR LAWRENCE: "Hold, then. Go home, be merry. Give consent To marry Paris. Wednesday is tomorrow. Tomorrow night look that thou lie alone. Let not the Nurse lie with thee in thy chamber. (Shows her a vial). Take thou this vial, being then in bed, And this distilled liquor drink thou off, When presently through all thy veins shall run A cold and drowsy humor, for no pulse Shall keep his native progress, but surcease. No warmth, no breath shall testify thou livest. The roses in thy lips and cheeks shall fade To paly ashes, thy eyes' windows fall Like death when he shuts up the day of life. Each part, deprived of supple government, Shall, stiff and stark and cold, appear like death. And in this borrowed likeness of shrunk death Thou shalt continue two and forty hours, and then awake as from a pleasant sleep."

27   "The fact is that it is not the same with dispositions as with sciences and faculties. It seems that the same faculty or science deals with two opposite things; but a disposition or condition which produces a certain result does not also produce the opposite results (οὐδὲ γὰρ τὸν αὐτὸν ἔχει τρόπον ἐπί τε τῶν ἐπιστημῶν καὶ δυνάμεων καὶ ἐπὶ τῶν ἕξεων. δύναμις μὲν γὰρ καὶ ἐπιστήμη δοκεῖ τῶν ἐναντίων ἡ αὐτὴ εἶναι, ἕξις δ' ἡ ἐναντία τῶν ἐναντίων οὔ...)" (*Eth. Nic.*, 1129a11–15). This teaching has a parallel in the *Metaphysics* where each one acts not at random but according to its desire. "Therefore everything which is rationally capable, when it desires something of which it has the capability, and in the circumstances in which it has the capability, must do that thing (ὥστε τὸ δυνατὸν κατὰ λόγον ἅπαν ἀνάγκη, ὅταν ὀρέγηται οὗ ἔχει τὴν δύναμιν καὶ ὡς ἔχει, τοῦτο ποιεῖν)" (*Metaphysics* 9, 1048a13–15).

The truth is that Aristotle supplies us in his *Poetics* with the fundamental theoretical apparatus to understand such an alteration of character, the mimetical σπουδαῖος being gradually refashioned by the tragic course of events. This is not only notionally intelligible in itself, but concretely observable in actual poetry and sometimes in life.

We could take as a striking example of this the eponymous Othello in Shakespeare's *Othello*, who at first appears perfectly in control and imperturbable, both courageous and straightforward in civic affairs and yet careful and mild in his private interactions with his cherished wife Desdemona. But slowly, through the perfidious insinuations and machinations of the diabolic Iago, which seep down into some previously undetected weakness of Othello's general personality, the irreproachable character will at the end of the play debase himself entirely and turn into an irrational maniac and assassin.

More in resonance this time with Aristotle's own surroundings, the character of Pentheus in Euripides' *Bacchae* is another fine example of an important reversal of personality in the process of a narrative development. There, the rational and self-controlled Pentheus is literally stood on his head and transformed into a transvestite by Dionysius: "Let us punish him. First drive him out of his wits, send upon him a dizzying madness, since if he is of sound mind he will not consent to wear women's clothing, but driven out of his senses he will put it on" (850–853).

If what is irrational, as Aristotle acknowledges, "is that from which amazement arises most" (1460 a12–13), and if what is amazing is in itself pleasant, than logically the irrational is in poetry the primary source of pleasure and delight. To the objectivity of truth, Aristotle opposes then an authentic enjoyable aesthetical experience.[28]

The real genius of Aristotle's experiment in the whole *Poetics* is to keep a constant balance—sometimes putting more weight on one aspect, sometimes more on the other—between two opposing requirements: (1) the need for consistency, regularity and plausibility in the interconnecting of the elements of the plot,[29] taking into consideration the characters individually and collective-

---

28 Of course, the degree of leeway one can in fact allow in poetry is a matter impossible to settle in advance since it depends on several factors, such as the style and personality of the poet himself, the literary genre to which his composition belongs (tragedy, comedy, novel, etc.) and the habits and customs prominent at such and such a point in historical time. Aristotle himself, appropriately, gives no quantifiable indication as to the amount of flexibility and freedom we should concede to the poet.

29 In this sense, the "necessity" of which Aristotle speaks in poetical composition, as one can observe in many passages (1451a9–15; 22–29; b34–35; 1452a18–21; 22–24; 1454a35–36), has definitely to do with the causal links between the elements of the plot, as opposed to

THE *POETICS* OF ARISTOTLE AND THE PROBLEM OF LITERARY LEEWAY   85

ly involved in the narrative; and (2) the need to produce pleasure (the recourse to music and scenery being important for Aristotle in this context),[30] to strike the imagination and surprise the public by all sorts of means, that is by way of exaggerations, marvels and paradoxes, through reversals of events, representations of uncommon characters either sublime and inspirational (tragedy) or ridiculous and despicable (comedy), who may undergo sudden transformations of behaviour, as we already observed.

And precisely because the poetic representation of existence escapes the day-to-day reality and its standard ordering, it has the ability to illuminate unexpected areas of the human condition. But what does it mean to *illuminate the human condition*? Here one must be very precautious in his evaluation of the instructive capacity of the poetic. Poetry shows us not what *should be done* (which is an ethical task) but what *could happen* in a multifaceted and sometimes capricious and unpredictable reality. In this sense, I would not subscribe to V. Goldschmidt's famous view according to which "Tragedy is more philosophic than philosophy itself: it is able to make intelligible accidental being."[31] I think myself that in Aristotle's view, the accident cannot be *explained* in any way whatsoever, not even through poetic discourse. Instead, the accident can only be *shown*, that is be put in front of the eyes for contemplation and appreciation, as a sort of mirror of possible human condition. Yes indeed, poetry is more philosophical than history, in that it shows freely different types of possible characters and series of events, but in such a variety that it is impossible to draw some definite lesson or rule from them. As we saw, its proper aim, or *orthotes*, is never to become prescriptive in the manner in which ethical discourse is.

---

    what Riu surprisingly suggested, when he writes that: "The necessary, instead of referring to causal connection, concerns the nobility that defines the character..." (206).

30 "Tragedy has all the elements of the epic—it can even use the hexameter— and in addition a considerable element of its own in the spectacle and the music, which make the pleasure all the more vivid" (26, 1462 a 14–17, translation Fyfe).

31 Cf. Goldschmidt 1982: "What is tragedy? Tragedy attempts to do what no science is capable of succeeding at: providing a knowledge of what happens by chance and doing so by deploying the very instruments of science: the quest for the universal. Tragedy represents destiny as the outcome of a sequence that is entirely accessible to reason. We can understand that Aristotle can consider it as 'more philosophic' than history...: in a sense tragedy is more philosophical than philosophy itself: it is *able to make intelligible accidental being*" (265, italics added). It is clear that Goldschmidt can only talk of a "knowledge of what happens by chance" and "making intelligible accidental being" by an equivocation and by lending "quest for the universal" a meaning that does not apply in poetry.

The poetical universals are only *possible universals*, possible general pictures of the world; they cannot be made equivalent to standard scientific universals. The meaning of the so-called universals in *Poetics* 9 is a well-known locus of interpretative conflict.[32] According to some,[33] the universals come close to being 'universal truths' or 'general truths' about human nature. For others, they are closer to a simple draft, sketch or scenario, as emerges when you read the passage of chapter 9 in connection with chapter 17, 1454a35 and following.[34] Since poetry admits of exceptions, exaggerations, unpredictable changes or evolutions of characters, since what is portrayed is not simply the ordinary man but the paradigmatic and the exceptional one, since what is depicted is not necessarily as it is supposed in all truth to be, but rather is "as it should be" (1060b33), or as the *doxa* pretends it to be (1461a1), or as it was used in the past to be (1461a3), the poetical universal offers a larger spectrum of possibilities than is to be expected in other (more or less predictable) spheres of knowledge.[35] Of course, as Janko rightly noticed, poetry is more universal "because it gives us a more generalized view of human nature and action than does history; it tells us what people of a certain type are likely to do or must do in a particular set of circumstances."[36] Yet, the 'types' in question are subjected to so many modifications, deviations and hypertrophic transpositions, that no strict conclusion for the direction of one's life can be directly mapped out from them.

Poetry does not *teach us* what to do as such, but it does nonetheless *show us* what could be the results of certain actions that are undertaken,[37] causing us—through multiple illustrative cases—both to react emotively and to reflect on the multiple facets of human conduct and conditions represented, thus

---

32 There is a good review of the literature on the subject in Armstrong 1998, 449–451, and Halliwell 2002, 193–206.

33 This is the reading (influenced by romanticism, cf. Halliwell 1987, 23 *sq.*) e.g., of Woodruff 1992, 86–88; Lucas 1968, 120); Butcher 1951, 163 and 194.

34 This is the reading, e.g., of Dupont-Roc/Lallot, Janko, and Halliwell (2002). At 1455b7–8, the καθόλου is conceived as a parallel to the story (*muthos*), a text which was subject to the stricture of Christ, followed by Kassel, and differently by Düntzer, followed by Tarán/ Gutas. But the reading of the MSS, excluded "un po'arbitrariamente" (Guastini), is justly re-established by Dupont-Roc/Lallot, Janko, Guastini, etc.

35 It "explore[s] possibilities of reality" as Halliwell 2002, 203, puts it.

36 Janko 1987, 91.

37 In French, I formulate this opposition by saying that poetry "n'enseigne pas (does not teach us) ce qu'il faut faire" but "nous renseigne (gives us information) sur ce qui peut arriver."

contributing, in this sort of loose and open way, to our cultural-moral-humanistic education.[38]

---

38   I would like to sincerely thank Christopher Sauder for his careful translation of this essay, and Francis Lacroix for his patient revision of the manuscript. I am grateful also to the anonymous reader appointed by the BACAP committee for his or her thoughtful remarks on my text, which I tried to take into account as much as I could, and to my learned commentator, Professor J. Aultman-Moore. His observations notwithstanding, I maintain my thesis. Aristotle concedes to the poets—and by extension to the arts in general—a freedom of expression that has no equivalent in any field of knowledge. Poetical correctness must be evaluated on the poetical level, a possibility for which Aristotle argues theoretically. This of course in no way implies that poetry is entirely cut off from the ethico-political domain. I showed that this literary leeway is already observable—both in plot construction and in the representation of characters—in tragedies, i.e. in the most difficult case; consider by contrast the situation in comedy, where the norms are less restrictive! Aristotle is the unremitting advocate of the right to fictionality, of the legitimacy of fiction, whether or not this vision may appear 'romantic'—after all, Romantics are not always wrong.

COLLOQUIUM 3

Commentary on Narbonne

J. Aultman-Moore
Waynesburg University

Abstract

In this response, I dispute Professor Narbonne's thesis on the literary leeway of the poet, emphasizing the constraints on poetic license from both the nature of the genre and the ethical and educational role tragedy played for Aristotle in civic life.

Keywords

tragedy poetry – plot– probability and necessity – literary leeway –character

Professor Narbonne presents us with an interesting and challenging account of Aristotle's position on the nature and practice of poetry. He invites us to consider whether Aristotle's conception of the poet and his or her art is not as prescriptive as is conventionally supposed. I cannot address all of the many avenues of inquiry he opens up for us in his paper, but I would like to address a few of them as they relate to the central themes of his paper.

According to Narbonne, the poet, like the painter Zeuxis, has "real creative leeway" in that he has the power to present his characters as greater than they are in order to represent such things as could happen (οἶα ἂν γένοιτο, *Poetics* 1451a36–38), indeed, as he puts it, "... with an even greater license, that which *should be*, in other words, that which the poet himself *wishes to see happen*" (2). Narbonne says that Aristotle's account of poetry in *Poetics* is *sui generis* and has no explicit dependence on the other theoretical or practical sciences of his work. The poet's art, says Narbonne, is more than just a "passive reproduction" but is a power to transfigure and transform. Thus, poetry does not suffer from the Platonic strictures of composition enunciated in the *Republic* where "correctness" is determined by an external standard of transcendent Truth, but enjoys a certain autonomy and is properly evaluated by norms internal to its own nature. In the interests of emphasizing the poet's creative freedom over the limits set by the nature of the poetic craft, he asserts that Aristotle's poetics is

COMMENTARY ON NARBONNE

"in no way naturalist in intention" (5–6). While sympathetic to post-Kantian Romantic developments in the understanding of artistic process with its emphasis on the poet's creative genius and powers of transformation, Narbonne's reading of Aristotle's poetics strikes me as anachronistic. This is so because much of Aristotle's discussion of tragic drama centers on the essential nature of the art and its relation to civic life, that is, to the audience experiencing this art form. Presenting the poetic craft as wholly constituted by the native powers of the poet unmoored from guidance by its essential nature or social and ethical context is alien to Aristotle's project.

Narbonne's claim, above, that Aristotle's account of poetry is not "naturalist in intention" seems opposed to his plain statement that poetry came into being from two causes, both of them rooted in our nature (αἰτίαι δύο τινὲς καὶ αὗται φυσικαί, *Poetics* 1448b4–5). First, Aristotle tells us that imitation is naturally implanted in us from childhood (τό τε γὰρ μιμεῖσθαι σύμφυτον τοῖς ανθρώποις ἐκ παίδων ἐστί, *Poet.* 1448b5–6), since human beings are the most imitative of other animals (τῶν ἄλλων ζῴων ὅτι μιμητικώτατον ἐστι, *Poet.* 1448b7), and such imitations are how we take our first steps towards learning. Secondly, he says that all human beings delight in such imitations (τὸ χαίρειν τοῖς μιμήμασι πάντας, *Poet.* 1448b8–9).

Narbonne's account is also opposed to the summary sketch of the "coming of age" of tragic drama that Aristotle provides at the beginning of the *Poetics*. Aristotle views the birth of tragedy as having a certain trajectory of growth and development toward a τέλος like any other natural organism (for example, Aeschylus's increasing the number of actors from one to two; Sophocles adding a third actor and introducing scene painting, *et cetera*). He says that, "after it underwent many changes, tragedy stopped, since it had attained its own nature (καὶ πολλὰς μεταβολὰς μεταβαλοῦσα ἡ τραγῳδία ἐπαύσατο ἐπεὶ ἔσχε τὴν αὑτῆς φύσιν" (*Poet.* 1449a14–15). Extending his biological ontology to culture, Aristotle holds that the tragic art has an essential nature and, as such, has intelligible principles and a purpose it must realize if it is to fulfill its nature and function. Thus, a credible plot-structure constructed according to probability or necessity, aimed at arousing fear and compassionate grief leading to a κάθαρσις of these emotions is the εἶδος of tragedy. The definitive form tragedy eventually assumed is just the place where the genre and poet could, together, achieve its greatest power and purpose. They are the constraints on practitioners of the art, thus limiting leeway. Still, constraints are not necessarily a straitjacket and Aristotle's prescriptive approach is somewhat open and flexible, making for multiple realizations. Viewed differently, Aristotle himself might suggest that his prescriptive approach is liberating and not constraining in the same way that the "constraints" of the moral virtues and φρόνησις free a person to flourish. On this take, Narbonne's interest in "leeway" as poetic license may be a later, Romantic preoccupation since Aristotle would view his somewhat "formulaic" framework as *enabling* the poet to realize the potentialities of the genre, not as a hindrance.

Professor Narbonne argues that in his discussion of tragic drama, Aristotle's emphasis on πρᾶξις over ἦθος is due to his interest in the way that "action makes something new out of the initial character, transforms it and imparts to it an unanticipated dimension." He contends that Aristotle has given the poet sufficient license to include characters that "can deviate immensely from normal behavior since the poetic environment is in no way normal itself." Since virtue is a disposition of character that is not easily lost, it is not in accord with necessity or probability, says Narbonne, that Hector will abandon his courage and run from Achilles in *Iliad* XXII. But Aristotle states that the poet should be granted this license because the scene is "more striking" (ἐκπληκτικώτερον, 1460b25) and, paradoxically, brings pleasure (1460a17–18) even as it exemplifies "the tragic destiny of Troy and the unjust collapse of its entire civilization...."

Narbonne seems to advocate a freeing of tragic drama from the strictures of having to represent character of a certain type when he says that "ethics can conform with what is expected from characters, but poetics cannot; in other words, the ethical *spoudaios* and the poetical *spoudaios* are not the same and must be clearly distinguished." While it is true, as we said above, that poetry is not to be limited to a rigid, external standard of correctness, this does not justify the claim that, for Aristotle, there is little or no connection between character as portrayed in tragedy and character as the subject of ethics. The very term, σπουδαῖος, is a central concept of the *Nicomachean Ethics* connoting the sort of person devoted to actualizing the peculiarly human excellences of moral virtue and practical wisdom. It seems clear that Aristotle has in mind a particular kind of character, and a plot-structure aimed at evoking the tragic emotions. The nexus and interplay of these three elements has ethical dimensions because the poet shows, among other things, the intelligibility of the protagonist's failure in his human quest to flourish. For example, Aristotle says that the portrayal of good men (ἐπιεικεῖς ἄνδρας, 1452b34) changing from prosperity to affliction does not evoke fear nor compassionate grief, but is only repulsive (μιαρόν ἐστιν, 1452b36); the wicked should not be portrayed going from affliction to prosperity because this is the most untragic of all, *et cetera*. In short, there is an in-built limitation on the kind of character that is the subject of tragedy and what that character may undergo within the plot-structure. The figure most suited to the evocation of the tragic emotions, says Aristotle, is someone who is good, but not pre-eminent in virtue, someone the audience can, in part, identify with because he is afflicted with a certain ἁμαρτία that will

COMMENTARY ON NARBONNE

bring suffering in its train. This is formulaic, to be sure, and it conflicts with Narbonne's emphasis on the creative autonomy of the poetic art and artist, but Aristotle does not conceive the craft as autonomous since it has a certain nature and work/function that can only be realized in certain ways. There may be other ways of writing a tragedy, but it seems that those which fail to conform to his general outline would be regarded as more or less "dysfunctional."

Professor Narbonne argues that, for Aristotle, action is a central component of tragic drama because of its power to "remold or partially modify an initial character, rather than it being the character that, as a preset component, would determine the narrative from the outset." The action of the drama "makes something new out of the initial character, transforms it and imparts to it an unanticipated dimension." Thus, Narbonne emphasizes how tragic drama depicts characters vulnerable to transformation or disfigurement through the plot-structure. Their character is not, for the most part, an unyielding type. Again, I would say that this is too bold and too bald a claim given the clear strictures on the successful realization of the tragic art that Aristotle provides. However, with the above qualifications in mind, I would be in basic agreement with this assertion. Still, it seems to me that Aristotle is as interested in the transformative effects of tragedy on the *audience* as he is on the action's effects on the protagonist. In part, he defines the nature of tragedy in relation to the emotional experiences of an audience, which are tied, in turn, to his understanding of moral judgment and education. All this is to say that while the poet enjoys a certain limited "leeway" his art cannot for Aristotle be defined in isolation from the social, political, ethical, and religious dimensions of the πόλις.

I have stated above that Aristotle has a more or less prescriptive understanding of tragedy, but this is not to say that tragedies which don't conform to the standard should be censored on ethical grounds as in Plato's καλλίπολις. Tragic poetry, according to Aristotle, should aim at enlarging an audience's sympathies through suffering identification with a fallible protagonist, one close enough to them to provoke φόβος but distant enough to evoke ἔλεος. This experience, he holds, will be cathartic, community-building, and ethically significant. Not that Aristotle is proposing a crudely instrumental relation of art to the city, but he means to show what this genre of drama can do and must do if it is to realize its nature.

Aristotle's interest in how poetry affects us emotionally is the reason why he sees it as ethically important. Ἔλεος and φόβος are not (*pace* Plato) irrational responses, but intelligent and intelligible reactions to a well-structured μῦθος. The emotional response and its aftermath, κάθαρσις, is central to the purpose of tragedy. What is the purpose of κάθαρσις? I will boldly go where scores have gone before! I think that Aristotle holds that the tragic art has, in part, an educational function. In his *Ethics*, Aristotle maintains that the accompanying pleasure or pain we feel in our actions is a sign of the state of our character-disposition (ἕξις). Delighting or being pained at the right things is a sign of ὀρθὴ παιδεία. Tragic representation arouses fear and pity as an *appropriate* emotional response to what is witnessed on stage. Virtue does not consist in eradicating the emotions but in shaping them to be existentially ready for excellent action. Thus, on this reading, κάθαρσις as the elimination of emotional response cannot be correct. Aristotle's understanding of the emotions as cognitive is acknowledged when he claims that the artistic experience of the downfall of a good man is rejected as *inappropriate* to the arousal of ἔλεος and φόβος. The experience of tragedy aligns our emotions with the moral and aesthetic judgments we make about the world. It is an emotional pedagogy for the audience. Aristotle and Plato agree on this, though of course Plato objects to this form of education for καλλίπολις. Experiencing the arousal and release of the tragic emotions, communally, is a personal and civic education. It is not a childish clasping of our collective wound and wailing, but a schooling in the intelligibility, such as there is, of how life can veer. Thus, tragic drama has not only standards internal to the genre, but a political and ethical dimension which, while not bringing down the hammer of censorship, limits the creative leeway of the poet.

COLLOQUIUM 3

Narbonne/Aultman-Moore Bibliography

Apostle, H.G., tr. 1984. *Nicomachean Ethics*, Grinnell, IA: Peripatetic Press.

Armstrong, J.M. 1998. Aristotle on the Philosophical Nature of Poetry. *The Classical Quarterly*, 48: 447–455.

Butcher, S.H. 1951 (1907). *Aristotle's Theory of Poetry and Fine Arts*. New York: Courier Corporation.

Donini, P. 2003. Mimèsis Tragique et Apprentissage de la Phronèsis. *Les Études philosophiques*, 4:436–450.

Dupont-Roc R. and J. Lallot, tr. 1980. *Aristote, La Poétique*. Paris: Seuil.

Frede, D. 1992. Twofold task of combining the unusual and the likely. In *Essays on Aristotle's Poetics*, ed. A.O. Rorty, 197–219. Princeton: Princeton University Press.

Gastaldi, S. 1987. Lo 'spoudaios' arristotelico tra etica e poetica. *Elenchos* 8:63–104.

Goldschmidt, V. 1982. *Temps physique et temps tragique chez Aristote*. Paris: Vrin.

Halliwell, S., tr. 1987. *The Poetics of Aristotle, translation and commentary*. Chapel Hill: University of North Carolina Press.

Halliwell, S., tr. 1998. *Aristotle's Poetics*, 2nd ed. Chicago: University of Chicago Press.

Halliwell, S. 2002. *The Aesthetic of Mimesis. Ancient Texts and Modern problems*. Princeton: Princeton University Press

Heath, M. 1991. The Universality of Poetry in Aristotle's Poetics. *The Classical Quarterly* 41: 389–402.

Janko, R., tr. 1987. *Aristotle Poetics I, with The Tractatus Coislinianus, A hypothetical Reconstruction of poetics II, The Fragments of the On Poets*. Indianapolis/Cambridge: Hackett.

Kristeller, P.O. 1951. The Modern System of the Arts: A Study in the History of Aesthetics Part I. *Journal of the History of Ideas* 12: 496–527.

Lucas, D.W., tr. 1968. *Aristotle, Poetics*. Oxford: Oxford University Press.

Riu, X. 2011. Le nécessaire, l'*eikos* et la causalité dans la *Poétique*. In *La causalité chez Aristote,* eds. L. Couloubaritsis and S. Delcominette, 178–206. Paris: Vrin.

Roberts, R.W., tr. 1984. Rhetoric. In *The Complete Works of Aristotle*, ed. J. Barnes, Princeton: Princeton University Press.

Romilly, J. de. 1968. *Time in Greek Tragedy*. Cornell: Cornell University Press.

Schmitt, A., tr. 2011. *Aristoteles, Poetik*. Berlin: Akademie Verlag.

Shepper, G., ed. 1965. *Philip Sidney's Defence of Poesy* (1580). Manchester: Manchester University Press.

Shield, C., tr. 2016. *Aristotle: De Anima*. Oxford: Oxford University Press.

Gutas, D., and L. Tarán, tr. 2012. *Aristotle, Poetics*. Leiden/Boston: Brill.

Woodruff, P. 1992. Aristotle on *mimesis*. In *Essays on Aristotle's Poetics*, ed. A.O. Rorty, 73–96. Princeton: Princeton University Press.

COLLOQUIUM 4

A Man of No Substance: The Philosopher in Plato's *Gorgias*

S. Montgomery Ewegen
Trinity College

Abstract

At the center of Plato's *Gorgias*, the shameless and irascible Callicles offers an attack against philosophy (484c and following). During this attack, he describes philosophy as a pastime fit only for the young which, if practiced beyond the bloom of youth, threatens to render those who practice it politically inept and powerless. Moreover, when taken too far, philosophy provokes the city into stripping the philosopher of all of his rights and property, leaving him with no οὐσία at all (486c). Thus, according to Callicles, far from making one powerful within the city, philosophy ultimately renders one impotent and utterly without substance. In what follows I argue that the Socrates of the *Gorgias* agrees with this characterization of the philosopher as the one who lacks power and οὐσία. However, whereas Callicles sees such a condition as the most worthless and pitiable sort, Socrates sees it as the unique and singular posture from out of which true philosophical thinking, and true political power, are possible. As I will show, through the course of the *Gorgias* as a whole, Socrates offers a counter-discourse that presents the philosopher as a powerless person lacking οὐσία who is precisely thereby able to undertake a pursuit of the truth and the good. Phrased otherwise: Socrates takes ignorance understood as lack or powerlessness to be the very condition for the possibility of philosophy and true political power, while showing rhetoric understood as the pretense of wisdom to be an obstruction to these.

Keywords

power – rhetoric – retreat – *parrhesia* – Socrates

From its very beginning, the *Gorgias* is concerned with the question of *power*.[1] After having arrived late for Gorgias's rhetorical display, Socrates enunciates his reason for having come to see Gorgias: namely, he wishes to discover "the power (ἡ δύναμις) of the skill of that man" (447c). Indeed, Socrates' entire inquiry is directed toward power; and in what follows we will see that Socrates' questioning is not restricted narrowly to the power of Gorgias's skill nor the power of rhetoric, nor even to the power of philosophy, but is rather directed toward the very nature of δύναμις itself. By the end of the *Gorgias*, one finds a radical inversion on the part of Socrates of the traditional understanding of power, and it is the principle task of this paper to illuminate and analyze the character of this inversion.

As he begins to converse with Gorgias, Socrates seeks to understand the power (δύναμις, 450e) of rhetoric and wishes to know over what, precisely, it has authority (κῦρος, 451d). As is immediately revealed, rhetoric in fact consists of nothing other than an exercise of a certain kind of power and authority. Gorgias states that rhetoric has power and authority over that which is "responsible for freedom among human beings themselves and ... for ruling over others in one's own *polis*" (452e). Amplifying a bit, Gorgias claims that rhetoric consists in the ability to persuade (πείθειν) others in political matters, further asserting that

> it is by means of this power (τῇ δυνάμει) that you will have the physician and trainer as your slaves. As for the moneymaker, he'll be making all that money for somebody other than himself—namely, for you, the one who has the power (τῷ δυναμένῳ) of speaking and persuading the many. (452e; translation modified. In this paper, I have relied on three translations [see bibliography]. I tend to favor the Loeb, but often the Arieti was superior, though sometimes with my modifications.)

One sees here that rhetoric, for Gorgias, is the power of persuading others, of lording over them, by means of λόγος: it is the very power, then, of exerting power over others. Rhetoric is the δύναμις of wielding δύναμις and κῦρος over others by means of λόγος. As Socrates glosses it, "you say that rhetoric does nothing more than produce (ποιεῖν) persuasion in the audience" (453a). Rhetoric thus *makes* or *manufactures* (ποιεῖν) persuasion within those at whom it is directed. Much like a demiurge works his hammer upon stone, shaping it into whatever form he wills, the rhetorician works his words upon the audience, persuading them of whatever he wishes.[2] Rhetoric is a technique for the willful

---

1 See Haden 1992, 313. See also Saxonhouse 1983: "The *Gorgias* is not simply about rhetoric vs. philosophy as a way of life. It is also about different kinds of power" (166).

2 See Haden 1992, 320, who talks about such persuasion in terms of 'assimilation.'

A MAN OF NO SUBSTANCE: THE PHILOSOPHER IN PLATO'S *GORGIAS* 97

exercise of power over another, and the rhetorician is the craftsman (δημιουργός) wielding such power (453a).[3] Phrased otherwise: rhetoric is a technology of power.

Immediately after the power of rhetoric has come to light, Socrates makes a statement to which we must attend closely: for it points to a subtle counter-discourse underway within the *Gorgias* both at the level of the conversation and of the action. Socrates says that, although he *suspects* he knows what Gorgias means by defining rhetoric as the power to persuade, he does not yet *clearly know* what he means. Owing to this ignorance, Socrates says that he will ask Gorgias to clarify "not for your sake, but for the sake of the λόγος, in order that it go forward (προΐη) as much as it can and make clear to us what is being spoken (λέγεται) about" (453c). Rather than offering his own opinion on the matter, then, Socrates aims to let the λόγος itself unfold in whatever way it will. Thus, just after Gorgias has defined rhetoric as the power to persuade others and lord over them, Socrates effectively withdraws *his self* and its opinions from the conversation, distancing himself from the sort of rhetorical position that Gorgias has just described—for by retreating away from making a claim of his own, and by instead making way for the λόγος, Socrates makes it impossible in what follows for him to persuade Gorgias of anything. Thus, in the face of a rhetoric essentially comprised of a will to power over others, Socrates withdraws from such a will to power, yielding instead to the unraveling of the λόγος.

This gesture of withdrawal continues to unfold as the conversation progresses. In an effort to problematize and ultimately clarify Gorgias's definition of rhetoric, Socrates articulates certain other arts that also work upon others by means of persuasion, namely, any art that is *taught*: for whosoever teaches, as Gorgias affirms, also persuades (453d). What is especially striking is the manner in which Socrates here offers *in deed* a counter-definition of teaching that does not at all operate by means of persuasion. In keeping with his gesture of withdrawal indicated above, Socrates does not attempt in these pages to persuade Gorgias of anything: that is, he does not attempt to exert his 'work' upon Gorgias. Instead, Socrates *asks questions* of Gorgias, questions that allow Gorgias the space in which his own λόγος can unfold. One sees this in the following statement of Socrates':

> it is for the sake of progressing through the λόγος in an orderly way that I ask, not for your sake—but so we don't get used to guessing and

---

3 See McCoy 2008: "… words can persuade others to shift their opinions. Gorgias gives *logoi* almost unlimited power in this regard: words can change both the emotions and the opinions of those who hear them, essentially enslaving the listener to the power of the speaker" (90).

snatching ahead of time what is said from each other, but so you may progress through your own [thoughts] as you wish (βούλῃ), according to your own underlying view. (454c)

Thus, precisely in that moment when he is coming to understand Gorgias's pedagogical approach as a persuasive working of one's will upon another, we see Socrates practicing by contrast a kind of *midwifery* whereby he withholds his own view so as to allow the λόγος of the other to come to pass. Whereas rhetoric consists in the working of one's will upon another, this other way— Socrates' way—consists in placing one's own will in abeyance so that the λόγος can go where *it* will. Phrased otherwise: whereas rhetoric takes itself to have mastery over λόγος, Socrates' way yields to the λόγος in a receptive gesture. One notes in passing that Socrates' learned his maieutic practice from his mother (see *Theaetetus* 150 and following).

That Socrates is practicing such maieutics becomes clearer as the conversation progresses. Gorgias goes on to maintain that rhetoric is so powerful as to "gather all other powers under itself" (456a) and to make the rhetor "have the power (δυνατὸς) to speak against everyone about everything, so as to be more persuasive ... about anything he may wish (βούληται)" (457a–b). In response to this 'daimonic' power of rhetoric, Socrates makes the following statement:

> you seem to me now to be saying things that do not entirely ... harmonize with what you said at first about rhetoric. But I am afraid of refuting you, lest you take it as obvious that I am someone who is speaking as a lover of victory, not on the subject, but against you. And so, if you too are one of those men such as I, I will gladly question you thoroughly, but if you're not, I will leave you alone. And of what sort of person am I? One who would gladly be refuted if I should say something not true, and one who would gladly refute someone else should he say something not true, being no less gladly refuted than refuting. (457e–458b; translation modified)

Thus, over against Gorgias's understanding of rhetoric as the imposing of one's will upon the other in such a way as to enslave them, one finds with Socrates a complete surrendering of the will in the face of the λόγος so as to let the truth come to pass.[4] Through Socrates' manner of conducting himself with Gorgias,

---

4 By contrast, McCoy sees Socrates as seeking only to win his argument against Gorgias (McCoy 2008, 91). This seems to me to be in tension with the various disavowals that Socrates makes throughout his conversation, and especially with his claim that he is not a 'lover of victory.'

one finds *in deed* an epistemological and pedagogical comportment that runs counter to the one being offered *in speech* by Gorgias, a comportment that suspends the will in the face of the λόγος.[5]

This comportment, as a complete inversion of Gorgias's view regarding rhetoric, is grounded in a gesture of *self-effacement* or *self-erasure*. As Socrates has said, he is just as happy to be refuted as to refute. To be refuted is to withdraw one's own position in the face of the truth, to yield one's own opinion to the truth. Motivated not at all by a love of victory (φιλονικοῦντα), but rather by a love of the λόγος—that is, φιλοσοφία—Socrates is eager to withdraw his own opinion if it means that the truth will come to pass. In other words: rather than loving asserting his power willfully over others, Socrates loves being *overpowered* by the true λόγος. Thus, whereas Gorgias claims to possess a power capable of overpowering anybody on any subject, Socrates here articulates a gesture that yields to the λόγος, a gesture that makes a space in which the λόγος can assert itself. Insofar as it is an inversion of Gorgias's position—a position constituted by the will to power—one can say that Socrates' way consists of a *powerlessness* in the face of the λόγος.

This powerlessness can be seen in Socrates' famous predilection for proceeding in an interrogative mode: for when one asks questions, one demonstrates that one is in a position of epistemological poverty. To be sure, one sometimes, if not often, finds Socrates speaking in the form of assertions. Indeed, the Socrates of the *Gorgias* makes any number of apparent assertions, such as the claim, made during his conversation with Polus, that rhetoric is a form of pandering (462b–466a), a claim that one might be tempted to take as Socrates' 'own' over against the various assertions made by the other interlocutors. Yet, given Socrates' insistence within the *Gorgias* that he himself knows nothing about the matters under consideration, but rather speaks only as one who seeks (ζητῶ) (506a), by what right could one say that these assertions 'belong' to Socrates or somehow represent or express 'his' views? Indeed, given that such utterances are grounded in ignorance, by what right could one call them 'assertions' at all? In making such statements from out of a position of ignorance, Socrates in no way asserts them to be correct: rather, he posits them

---

5   Along similar lines, see Saxonhouse: "Rhetoric leads to domination over the opinions of others.... The desire for domination comes from a dissatisfaction with what one has, and a supposition that domination will lead to the fulfilment of some of those desires. Polus and Callicles give expression to what is to become the classic twentieth century formulation of politics—who gets what, where, when, and how. Socrates is to question that formulation of politics and the conception of power implicit in it" (Saxonhouse 1983, 166).

as positions to be assayed and assessed, tested and considered.[6] Even less so does Socrates *assert himself* in such statements, setting them forth as if they were *his views* to which others must of necessity adhere, as if he were an expert in possession of σοφός rather than one who, precisely because he lacks such σοφός, seeks it. Rather, by asking such questions from out of a posture of ignorance, Socrates reveals that he does not have a view of his own; or, rather, that his view is necessarily one of searching and questioning which, as lacking the truth toward which it is directed, is in no position to assert itself. Even if one were to attribute such statements to Socrates in a strong sense—something which, for the reasons mentioned immediately above, one cannot do—one would have to grant that they are views to which he does not feel particularly attached: for as Socrates has just said during his conversation with Gorgias, he is more than happy to see his statements refuted (458b). But what kind of *assertion* gleefully abandons its status as an assertion, making way for the ascendency of another? Socrates' ignorance, as well as his enthusiasm for being refuted, are opposed to the very nature of assertions and assertiveness. The statements that Socrates makes—statements which, grounded in ignorance, make no claim and assert no power—are more structurally akin to questions than they are to assertions. Even when he makes a statement, Socrates is posing a question.

Socrates now turns to a conversation with Polus, during which one sees an intensification of the inversion to the willfulness that characterized Gorgias's position. As was the case with Gorgias, one finds with Polus an understanding of rhetoric localized around the issue of the willful exercise of power;[7] and, as was the case with his conversation with Gorgias, one finds Socrates here offering a counter-discourse that serves to invert Polus's understanding of power. For Polus, power is the ability to do whatever one wishes (466c); for Socrates, power is the ability to do what is *just*, where this means the ability to set one's own wishes aside in order to follow what the λόγος shows to be just and good. For Polus, it is better to cause injustice than to suffer it (469b); for Socrates, it is far better to suffer injustice than to cause it to another. For Polus, it is wretched for the person acting unjustly to be caught (472d); for Socrates, this is the best

---

6   One apparent exception is Socrates' claim, made at 523a, that the μῦθος he is about to offer is 'true' (ἀληθῆ). However, as argued below, this passage in fact marks Socrates' deferral to a higher λόγος, and thus entails a personal disavowal of knowledge.

7   See Saxonhouse: "It is Polus' urge for power that drives him to follow Gorgias, that keeps him in close attendance to Gorgias, so that one day perhaps he may do more than simply articulate the role of rhetoric, that he may someday indeed exercise the power which rhetoric promises" (Saxonhouse 1983, 145).

A MAN OF NO SUBSTANCE: THE PHILOSOPHER IN PLATO'S *GORGIAS*　　　101

possible outcome for such a person, since acting unjustly with impunity is the
greatest sort of psychic sickness (479c). Thus, for each point Polus adduces regarding the value and power of rhetoric, Socrates offers an almost caricatured
counter-point, setting forth a starkly inverted notion of the traditional concept
of power.

What one must keep in mind in these pages is that, in keeping with his previously exhibited deference to the λόγος, Socrates is not offering *his own* opinions over against Polus's. Rather, it is precisely by withholding his own opinions
that Socrates is allowing the λόγος to unfold in such a way as to show the inadequacy of Polus's position. One sees this clearly when, having brought Polus to
the brink of contradicting himself, Socrates urges Polus to "present [himself]
nobly to the λόγος as though to a physician" (475d). Thus, it is not Socrates who
is refuting Polus here: rather, it is the λόγος that, through its unfolding, has
brought Polus to the place of contradiction. Socrates is not the doctor—the
λόγος is: and it is by submitting himself to the λόγος that Polus will be purged of
his false opinions. Owing to his sense of shame (487b), Polus indeed finally
yields to the λόγος, making way for the statements that stand in contradiction
to his original thesis.

So far we have seen Socrates, in surrendering his own will, making way for a
λόγος that has radically inverted the positions held by both Gorgias and Polus.
It is in light of this inversion that Callicles interrupts the conversation, asking
Socrates whether he is jesting or being serious is setting forth this inverted
(ἀνατετραμμένος) view (481c). One must attend closely to Socrates' response to
Callicles' question:

> do not be surprised at my saying [these things that have been said], but
> make my beloved philosophy stop speaking thus. For she, my dear friend,
> speaks what you hear me saying now …; philosophy always says the same,
> and it is her speech that now fills you with wonder. (482a–b)

Thus, in answer to Callicles' question about whether Socrates was jesting or
being serious during his engagement with Polus, one would have to say *neither*:
for, properly understood, Socrates himself has said nothing during that ex-
change. Rather, *philosophy itself* has been speaking. Socrates has retreated behind philosophy, withdrawing his self and its opinions from the conversation
so that philosophy may articulate itself. Thus, during his discourses with Gorgias and Polus, it was not by means of Socrates' argumentative power that the
traditional view of power got inverted, but rather by the power of the λόγος, a
power that can express itself *only because* Socrates yielded his own power in
the face of it. Socrates' suspension of his will, his retreat from offering his own

opinions, is the gesture that made possible a genuine reception of the philosophical λόγος.

It is at this point that Callicles begins his sustained attack against philosophy, a criticism that orients itself around the powerlessness of the philosopher. Callicles begins by attacking the notion that arose during Socrates' conversation with Polus that it is better to suffer injustice than to exert it upon another. Regarding such a situation, Callicles states that "[such suffering] is not even the experience of a *man* (ἀνδρὸς), but of some man-slave (ἀνδραπόδου) ... who is not himself able to help himself or another for whom he cares" (483a–b). Callicles continues to denigrate such slavishness, noting that it is such people—whom he calls "the weakest sort of people" (οἱ ἀσθενεῖς ἄνθρωποί, 483b) and "unmanly" (ἀνανδρία, 492b)—who formulated laws in the first place, laws that do nothing but seek to restrain those who are by nature more powerful (483b). These laws define the willful activities of the stronger as unjust, when in fact (according to Callicles) it is this very effort at restraining the strong that is unjust: for "nature itself reveals that it is just that the better have more than the worse and the more powerful (τὸν δυνατώτερον) more than the powerless (τοῦ ἀδυνατωτέρου)" (483d). Injustice is any attempt to prevent the powerful from being powerful; and justice is nothing but the exercise of power by the powerful accompanied by the will to further power.

Callicles continues his denigration of philosophy, again couching his criticism in explicitly gendered terms:

> You see ... it falls to this man [that is, the philosopher], even if he should have a very good nature, to become unmanly (ἀνάνδρῳ) and to flee (φεύγοντι) the affairs of the polis and the marketplaces ... and cower down (καταδεδυκότι) and spend the rest of his life whispering in a corner with three or four young fellows, and never to utter a free and great and adequate remark. (485d)

Given that philosophy is said by Callicles to make one less manly, one may presume that it (therefore) makes one more *womanly*, more *feminine*, where femininity would stand for the kind of weakness and submissiveness that so disgusts Callicles. Owing to this weakness, the philosopher would be unable to protect himself against others dragging him to court, accusing him unjustly, and having him put to death (486a–b): the philosopher, being weak, being feminine (for Callicles), would be at the mercy of those men wielding political power. In light of this, Callicles asks:

A MAN OF NO SUBSTANCE: THE PHILOSOPHER IN PLATO'S *GORGIAS*   103

> And how is this a wise thing, Socrates—any technical skill that takes a man of good nature and makes him worse, as one having the power (δυνάμενον) neither of helping himself nor of saving either himself or any other person from the greatest dangers, but leaves him stripped by his enemies of all his property (πᾶσαν τὴν οὐσίαν) and merely living without rights (ἄτιμον) in his polis? (486b–c)

Philosophy will lead its practitioner to be without property and without rights: much, it should be noted, as was quite nearly the actual state of affairs for women in Athens. The word translated above as 'property' is οὐσία. In its most pedestrian meaning, οὐσία means 'property,' 'estate,' or 'wealth.' In its more philosophical sense, the word οὐσία means 'that which is one's ownmost,' one's 'substance,' one's 'essence.' Understood in this way, Callicles is suggesting not just that philosophy will lead to material and political poverty but, much more severely, to an *ontological* poverty, a poverty of essence. The prolonged study of philosophy will lead, according to Callicles, to a degeneration of the substance of the practitioner: it will lead them not just *to have* nothing, but *to be* nothing. Callicles' use of the word ἄτιμος makes this clear. Translated above as 'without rights,' ἄτιμος essentially means 'without worth or value.' Callicles is asserting that philosophy renders the philosopher *worthless*: again, not just in a material or economic sense, but in an ontological one. The philosopher *is* worthless, *is* of null value: a real zero.

   Thus, according to Callicles, far from empowering or emboldening its practitioner, philosophy leaves that person impotent and utterly without value in the polis: it is a degenerative or corruptive procedure that robs its user of any οὐσία.[8] To have no οὐσία is to lack any discernable quality or set thereof that belongs to oneself, to possess nothing that could be called 'one's own,' to lack determinacy, to have no power by which to actualize one's self. In a word, to have no οὐσία is *to be* nothing, to lack a self, to lack *being*. In Callicles' view, philosophy, if practiced for too long, takes a man of good nature (εὐφυὴς) and renders him without nature: it turns a man into a non-being, a nothing, a non-self, a non-man—in Callicles view, therefore, something like a woman.

   On the surface, one can hardly imagine a harsher criticism of philosophy: philosophy, the pursuit that most of all concerns itself with true being, renders its practitioner utterly without being. One would of course expect Socrates to object vociferously to such a characterization of his beloved: and yet, instead of

---

8   "Philosophy, Socrates, is a charming thing, if someone engages with it moderately while young. But if a human being continues to waste time on it for too long, it will bring that person ruin (διαφθορά)" (484c).

contesting Callicles' harsh depiction of philosophy, Socrates appears to pay him a compliment:

> I now think that having met you I have happened upon a godsend. ... You see, I think that one who intends to test a soul adequately about living rightly must have three things all of which you have—knowledge, goodwill, and frankness (παρρησίαν). You see, I run into many people who are unable to test my soul because they are not wise, as you are. And while others are wise, they are not willing to tell me the truth because they don't care for me, as you do. (487a–c)

There is no doubt that Socrates' response here is ironic to some extent, and it is typical for scholars to treat is as such.[9] However, I would like to submit that Socrates is perfectly sincere here in his attribution of at least one of these qualities to Callicles: namely, his attribution to him of παρρησία, above translated as 'frankness.'[10] Yet, in attributing παρρησία to Callicles, Socrates is not complimenting him, but is rather marking the essential limitations of Callicles' understanding of rhetoric and, indeed, of power.[11] In order to see how this is so, it is necessary first to meditate on the ancient Greek notion of παρρησία.

In its most general sense, παρρησία refers to an openness and directedness in discourse, a license or freedom to say what one wants to say when one wants to say it. To quote Michel Foucault, who wrote extensively and insightfully on the role of παρρησία in antiquity,

> what is basically at stake in *parrhesia* is what could be called ... the frankness (la franchise), freedom, and openness that leads one to say what one has to say, as one *wishes* to say it (comme on a envie de le dire), when one *wishes* to say it (quand on a envie de le dire), and in the form *one thinks* (l'on croit) it is necessary for saying it. The term *parrhesia* is so bound up with the choice (le choix), decision (la décision), and attitude (l'attitude)

---

9   See, for example, Bourgault 2014, 72–73.

10   Ibid., 86: "... Callicles embodies precisely what characterizes bad *parrhesia* ... according to Plato". Against this, McCoy argues that it is Socrates who possesses παρρησία and Callicles who lacks it (McCoy 2008, 87). It is worth noting, however, that in the text it is Callicles, and not Socrates, who is said to possess it. One can claim that Socrates is being ironic here; but such a supposition misses, I think, Socrates' critical attitude toward παρρησία, an attitude which I elucidate below.

11   See Bourgault 2014, 66 who notes that *parrhesia* was sometimes used by Plato (as well as others) as a negative term.

A MAN OF NO SUBSTANCE: THE PHILOSOPHER IN PLATO'S *GORGIAS*   105

of the person speaking that the Romans translated it by, precisely, *libertas*. (Foucault 2001, 372; my emphasis)

Although this was not Foucault's point, one sees here that παρρησία is grounded in the desire (envie), the *will*, of the subject: it is about the subject saying what he wills when he wills it, and about the freedom that both makes possible and legitimates that will.[12] The person with παρρησία speaks freely,[13] speaks as he wishes and freely offers *his own* opinion about the matter. This implies that the person with παρρησία *has* an opinion *of his own*, as well as the confidence that his opinion is the truth. It is this confidence in the veracity of his own thinking that empowers the person with παρρησία to speak so directly and *in his own name*. Furthermore, one sees that παρρησία is a matter of *working* one's will upon another in order to convince them of one's position, a working-upon that Foucault casts in terms of the master/disciple relationship:

> Just as the disciple (le disciple) must keep quiet in order to bring about the subjectivation of his discourse, so the master's (le maître) discourse must obey the principle of *parrhesia* if, at the end of his action and guidance, he wants the truth of what he says to become the subjectivized true discourse of his disciple. (Foucault 2001, 366)

Παρρησία is thus a technique of *imposing* one's will upon another, of the master working his will upon the soul of the disciple. One sees this very clearly in the following passage from Foucault, and one would do well to note the gendered terms with which Foucault describes παρρησία:

> *Parrhesia* is the naked transmission (c'est la transmission), as it were, of truth itself. *Parrhesia* ensures in the most direct way this *para-dosis*, this transfer (ce transit) of true discourse from the person who already possess it to the person who must receive it, must be *impregnated* by it (qui doit s'en imprégner), and who must be able to use it and subjectivize it. (Foucault 2001, 382; my emphasis)

---

12   As Foucault writes elsewhere, "in *parrhesia*, the speaker makes it manifestly clear and obvious that what he says is his *own* opinion" (Foucault 2001, 12; my emphasis).

13   Foucault notes that *franc-parler*—'speaking freely'—is the preferred French translation of παρρησία (Foucault 2001, 373). As I hope to show presently, the speech of the philosopher is not 'free' at all, if this means the license to say whatever one wills. Rather, the speaking of the philosopher *submits* to the truth and is bound to it.

Παρρησία entails the transfer of truth from the subject to the object, the master to the disciple, a transfer that is above cast in overtly masculine terms. The master *disseminates* truth to the disciple who is there to (silently) receive it (Foucault 2001, 366), a receiving that one could imagine, following the gendered language employed by Foucault, to be feminine in structure. Thus, despite the fact that Foucault goes to great lengths to differentiate παρρησία from rhetoric (Foucault 2001, 368, 381), one sees that they in fact share the same essential structure: both are techniques of the will to mastery, the will to power. Like rhetoric, παρρησία is a matter of the master exerting power over, or even into, another: it is a technology of power.

Socrates soon ties such willful speaking to a kind of *shamelessness*.[14] As Socrates explains, Gorgias and Polus, owing to their senses of shame, lacked the παρρησία to say to Socrates what they really thought (487b). In his words, "the two of them, in fact, have come to such a degree of shamefulness that, though being ashamed, each of them was himself daring to say things *in opposition to himself* (αὐτὸς αὐτῷ ἐναντία λέγειν) while before many people" (487b). In other words, owing to their senses of shame and concomitant lack of παρρησία, both Gorgias and Polus were willing to yield their own positions to this λόγος, allowing it to overpower their wills. By contrast, Callicles—as the remainder of the *Gorgias* makes clear—lacks the shame required to allow such a yielding to occur.[15] His lack of shame and subsequent stubbornness in discourse is related directly to his possession of παρρησία. Owing to his willfulness in speech—owing, that is, to the manner in which his speaking always remains *his* speaking, and thus always remains an operation of his will—Callicles will never come to say anything opposite to what he *wills* to say. Callicles will forever speak in his own name, stubbornly confident in the veracity of his own opinions.

Παρρησία is thus not the courage to say what is true, as it is often presented: rather, it is a shamelessness that impels one only to say what one *thinks* is true *as if* it were the truth, a pretense that precisely *prevents* one from yielding to the truth. In the figures of Gorgias and Polus, and above all in Socrates, one sees moments where such pretense gives way to the λόγος, a giving-way that allows the λόγος to unfold where it will. In the figure of Callicles, by contrast, one finds no such making-way, no such reception: one finds instead the discourse of the man without shame, of the master, or rather, of the feigned

---

14   See Race 1979, 200.

15   See 495a. Bourgault argues that what Callicles lacks is not shame, but rather σωφροσύνη (Bourgault 2015, 72). I would submit that he lacks both and that, indeed, the two co-implicate one another.

A MAN OF NO SUBSTANCE: THE PHILOSOPHER IN PLATO'S *GORGIAS*   107

master, the one who thinks himself to be an authority who therefore has no reason to yield to anyone or anything. At the heart of Callicles' speaking, then, there is a willful assertion of self that serves as an impediment to truth: and the name Socrates gives to this impediment, at least within the confines of the *Gorgias*, is παρρησία.[16]

In the face of this analysis of παρρησία, I want to revisit Callicles' harsh denigration of philosophy that I quoted above. As Callicles had said,

> ... it falls to this man, even if he should have a very good nature, to become unmanly and to flee the affairs of the polis and the marketplaces ... and cower down and spend the rest of his life whispering in a corner with three or four young fellows, and never to utter a free and great and adequate remark. (485d)

Were one to inflect this passage differently in light of all that has been said above, one could say that philosophy leads one to become *unmanly*—that is, it leads one to drop the pretense and arrogant self-aggrandizement that so characterized Athenian masculinity and that characterizes Callicles' παρρησία. Further, philosophy leads one to retreat away from political affairs and the business of the *agora*[17]—a claim that Socrates himself makes in the *Theaetetus* when describing the philosopher (173c and following), as well as in the *Apology* when describing his own practice (36b and following). Moreover, philosophy leads one to whisper in a corner with a small group of people—rather than, for example, speaking abruptly and 'frankly' within a crowded courtroom while under the pressure of the water-clock. Finally, philosophy brings it about that its practitioner never utters "a free and great and adequate remark": that is, it brings it about that one, knowing oneself to be ignorant, never speaks one's own opinion as if it were adequate to the truth, as if it were sufficient, but instead withdraws one's own opinions in the face of a higher λόγος. So understood, one could say that Socrates' way of philosophy—a way that he has been depicting in both speech and deed throughout the *Gorgias*—agrees with

---

16   As scholars have noted, there is a tension between Socrates' apparent valuing of παρρησία and his own extensive use of irony, that is, of precisely *not* speaking freely and opening. See Bourgault 2015, 73. In his fascinating book on Plato's *Republic*, Stanley Rosen makes the following claim: "With all due recognition of irony and concealment, frankness is a necessary attribute of the Socratic, and so too of the Platonic, enterprise" (Rosen 2005, 283). One wonders, however, what sense 'frankness' can have for a person for whom irony and concealment are so integral.

17   See 447a, where Socrates blames his tardiness on Chaerephon's insistence that they spend time in the *agora*.

Callicles' depiction of it; or, rather, it agrees with the words with which Callicles describes it, while those words must be understood in an entirely different sense based upon the inverted understanding of power that the λόγος has brought about.[18]

Socrates continues to interrogate Callicles, granting him the space in which his own view regarding rhetoric, power, and political rule can unfold. After a while, Callicles grows taciturn and is unwilling to continue in the discussion (505c). This unwillingness is owed precisely to his παρρησία: that is, to his certainty of the veracity of his own thinking and his concomitant unwillingness to abandon his will. Unlike Gorgias and Polus before him, Callicles proves incapable of letting himself undergo the shame of being contradicted, an inability that belongs intimately to his understanding of power. Phrased otherwise: Callicles gives *up* by refusing to give *in*; he retreats *from* the λόγος by refusing to submit *to* the λόγος. Rather than yielding his position to the λόγος, Callicles, insistent as ever that he is right, withdraws from the conversation. Incapable of feeling shame, Callicles cannot surrender his self to the higher measure of the λόγος.[19] It is thus precisely his powerfulness—his *manliness*—that prevents him from yielding to the truth.[20]

Socrates, by contrast, is able to erase his self and let the λόγος unfold. This is evident in the following pages where Socrates, in the face of Callicles' withdrawal from the conversation, is forced to finish on his own. In a remarkable scene, Socrates stages a one-person dialogue, giving voice to a dialogical back-and-forth whereby the truth of Callicles' thesis that the good and the pleasant are the same is refuted. Prefacing this scene, Socrates says:

> I shall go through the λόγος as it seems to me to be; but if to any of you I don't seem to be saying things that agree with myself, it is necessary that you take hold of them and refute me. You see, I am not at all saying what

---

18   See Saxonhouse 1983, who notes the difference between Callicles' and Socrates' conceptions of power: "[The differences between Callicles and Socrates] stem from different conceptions of power, power over others as in the master and slave relationships of Callicles' vision, and power over oneself—as power to distinguish between good and bad passions and to choose the former" (166).

19   As Race 1979 astutely notes, what is truly shameful, for Socrates, is ignorance (i.e., feigned knowledge, and thus ignorance of one's own ignorance) (201). Callicles, in failing to feel shame, fails to see himself as ignorant: he fails to become aware of his own epistemological poverty.

20   See 494d: "According to you, Callicles, I dumbfounded Polus and Gorgias and made them feel shame, but *you* are not dumbfounded and you do not feel shame, on account of being so manly (ἀνδρεῖος)."

A MAN OF NO SUBSTANCE: THE PHILOSOPHER IN PLATO'S *GORGIAS* 109

> I am saying as one who knows, but I am seeking knowledge in common with you, so that, should the one who speaks discover something, going off in a different direction from me, I shall be the first one to agree with him. (505e–506a)

One must note that, in providing this one-person dialogue, Socrates is not replacing Callicles' position with his *own*. To the contrary, through staging such a *dialogical* scene Socrates places his own voice into abeyance, *listening* instead to the unfolding of the λόγος.[21] As the passage makes clear, this retreat is grounded in his knowledge of his own ignorance: for in knowing that he does not know, Socrates further knows that he himself has nothing authoritative to say about these matters. Rather, as one who is ignorant—as one who is therefore impoverished with respect to the truth of things—Socrates withdraws his own opinions so that he might submit to the authority of the λόγος. It is only because he knows himself to be without the truth that Socrates is capable of discovering it: it is thus only because of his *lack*, his impotency, that Socrates has the power to receive the truth.

During his one-person dialogue, Socrates allows the following λόγος to unfold: namely, that the pleasant and the good are not the same, as Callicles had claimed; that only the self-restrained soul is virtuous and good (507a), while the soul that wantonly pursues its every wish is bad (507a); that the one wishing to be happy must above all else flee (φευκτέον) wanton self-interest (507d) and strive toward "the power of acting in common" (507e), a power that Socrates calls a "geometric equality (ἡ ἰσότης ἡ γεωμετρική)" (508a). Such geometric equality is, at its core, nothing other than the power of restraining and yielding one's own desires in the face of the good of the polis as a whole, a making-way for the desires of the others with which one lives, an acting with a view toward the cosmos of which one is a part. Socrates notes that Callicles lacks this power, possessing instead great πλεονεξία: the arrogant and unbridled drive for the possession of *more*, what I would simply call 'the will to power' of which, as I showed above, παρρησία is an integral part.[22] Callicles is unable to live well and to be happy because of this will to power, this πλεονεξία,

---

21   See Bourgault 2014, 73–75 who offers an insightful and compelling argument regarding Socratic silence and Socratic listening.

22   See Saxonhouse 1983, 155: "Life for Callicles is the passionate life, a life of constantly seeking more; it is the Hobbesian life where one's desires can never be fully satisfied, only briefly met and then instantly reignited.... The real man is the eternal consumer." See also Zuckert 2009, 551: "As his disdain for moderation indicates, Callicles believes that the best thing for human beings is to be able to do what they want."

and the contiguous inability to yield his own desires in the face of the good of the polis as a whole. Only those who can so yield may live a happy life.[23]

What this means, of course, is that the politically powerful person as Callicles conceives him—that person of great strength and manliness (491b) who wields his power over the weak and does whatever he wills whenever he wills it (492c)—is unable to be happy owing precisely to this abundance of power. More crucially, such a person is unable *to rule* the city well, owing to his inability to rule himself by restraining his desire for the pleasant in the face of a λόγος regarding the good. Ruling oneself is nothing other than the effacing of the self and its desires in the face of a higher order, a deferential gesture to a larger cosmos ordered by the good and beautiful (507d–e). Somewhat paradoxically, then, the true ruler is the one who *most of all* is ruled by the truth: it is the one who surrenders authority and power to a greater whole. So understood, the one most capable of ruling would be the one with the least power, the least πλεονεξία, who is therefore most able to receive the truth of things. The power of ruling would consist in submission to the truth. But this means that the most powerful ruler is precisely the most powerless: namely, the one who yields one's own will entirely to the λόγος regarding what is best and most beautiful for the polis. By contrast, the one with the greatest capacity of exercising their will over others—the tyrant—would be the least powerful, the least capable of ruling well. True political power consists in powerlessness and submission to the truth.

In light of this, one can make sense of Socrates' claim that he is the only Athenian currently living who practices the true political art (ἀληθῶς πολιτικὴ τέχνη, 521d). Owing to the deferential gesture that stands at the heart of Socrates' practice, Socrates is able to place his own desires in abeyance and make way for a reception of the λόγος, a reception that will bring him into relation with the beautiful, the good, the true. It is this self-erasure—which is nothing other than Socratic ignorance—that makes possible a true assessment of what is best for the whole, for the ordered cosmos of which he is only

---

23   To be sure, Callicles accuses Socrates of a certain willfulness of his own: namely, of seeking only to refute him, of seeking to assert himself over the other interlocutors by dominating the argument (515b), and even of acting violently as he does so (505d). In other words, Callicles accuses Socrates of just the sort of will to dominate and overpower that Callicles himself possesses. This, however, is as it should be: for Callicles lacks the appropriate context in which to view Socrates' behavior as anything other than agonistic. For Callicles, for whom exerting power over others is a virtue, refutation is merely a rhetorical means by which one asserts oneself over another and dominates them. The idea that Socrates would be conversing with him for any reason other than victory is unthinkable for him.

A MAN OF NO SUBSTANCE: THE PHILOSOPHER IN PLATO'S *GORGIAS*

a part. It is thus his radical powerlessness—his weakness in the face of the λόγος—that renders Socrates uniquely capable of the true political art.[24]

One sees an expression of this powerlessness at the very end of the *Gorgias*. Having finished his one-person dialogue, Socrates offers Callicles a μῦθος regarding the fate of just and unjust souls after death, a μῦθος which Socrates insists is a true λόγος (523a) to which Callicles ought to submit. With the enunciation of this μῦθος one sees Socrates completely abandoning his authority in the face of the λόγος so as to allow the truth to become manifest (523a). Here are the closing words of the *Gorgias*:

> And so, let us follow the λόγος as our guiding authority (ἡγεμόνι), the one that now discloses itself, which shows to us that this is the best way of life, to live and die practicing both justice and the rest of excellence. And so let us follow this (ἐπώμεθα) and call on others to do so too, and let us not follow the way that you believe and call on me to follow—for you see, Callicles, it is worth nothing (οὐδενὸς ἄξιος). (527e)

Thus, for Socrates, it is not a human ruler at all who will lead human beings to the best life, and certainly not Socrates himself as some expert who possesses knowledge. Rather, it is the true λόγος itself that will lead them; and only the person who can make way for this λόγος, submitting to it, may live well.

With this ending one sees that Callicles' claim that philosophy renders one powerless and without οὐσία is entirely correct: yet, it is this place of nothingness, of pure receptivity, that allows one to make a place for the truth and (therefore) makes possible the genuine pursuit of the good life. By contrast, that position that Callicles set forth—the position of the man with δύναμις, with πλεονεξία, with παρρησία, the position of the tyrant—is worth nothing: and this nothingness is simply the final vapid expression of what we typically understand as *power*. If one yields to the λόγος, one sees that the will to power is powerless: it is unable to attain to truth or realize the human good. The most powerful way, by contrast, is the way of retreat, the way of withdrawal, the way

---

24 Though she does not express it in terms of powerlessness, it seems to me that Saxonhouse reaches a similar conclusion regarding Socrates' understanding of power: "The conception of power which Socrates proposes in this dialogue is not the power to fill another and satisfy her desires, nor to make another serve one's own interests. It is a conception of power which can only be understood in terms of making one better, and making one better consists in making one aware of what one *lacks*—not the dockyards or imports or other such filth—but virtue" (Saxonhouse 1983, 165; my emphasis).

that yields power and authority to the λόγος, a way of pure receptivity: true power consists in such powerlessness.[25]

One finds such powerlessness above all in the figure of Socrates; a figure of that one who, in knowing himself to be ignorant, retreats away from offering his own opinions, making way instead for a reception of the λόγος. In the powerless Socrates, one finds only a lack, an absence, a place of withdrawal; not, however, in the sense of an empty vapidity, but rather in the sense of an active and potent capacity to suspend his will so to make a place for the truth to come to pass: a power that, over against the manliness extolled and exemplified by Callicles, is presented within the *Gorgias* in feminine terms.[26] In Socrates, one finds a power that inverts, in the strongest possible terms, the manly willfulness characteristic of rhetoric and its motivating will to power.

Over against this characterization, one perhaps thinks of Socrates the gadfly—the radical provocateur who, through this practice of a novel form of *agon*, ceaselessly berates and admonishes his fellow Athenians. If one sees this as a moment where Socrates asserts his *self* and his *will* upon others, one overlooks that Socrates' entire philosophical exercise is grounded in a gesture of *reception* of, and *subservience* to, the god Apollo. Socrates was *attached* to the city by this god (*Apology* 30e): he is a *gift* from Apollo to Athens (*Ap.* 31a). Thus, Socrates' philosophical efforts of reproaching and exhorting the Athenians to examine themselves and live well is itself a kind of *suffering* on the part of Socrates: it is the *endurance* of a thing being done to him by the god (*Ap.* 23c.) Such a posture of endured reception requires a moment of self-erasure whereby Socrates suspends his own will and willfulness and defers to a higher λόγος. Such radical deference is the power of Socrates: a power that, owing to the manner in which it withdraws from the traditional notions of power and inverts them, must be understood as a kind of powerlessness.[27]

---

25   As Haden puts it somewhat differently: "It is by *surrendering* oneself to the lucidity of reason, which Callicles is unwilling to do, that one makes oneself authentically rational, i.e., an agent who identifies with reason and acts from it. That is Socratic power" (Haden 1992, 326; my emphasis).

26   See Strauss, who notes a certain kinship between Socrates and the classically feminine (Strauss 2004, 31–32).

27   My enduring gratitude to Dr. Robert Metcalf for reviewing an earlier draft of this paper and making extensive and extremely helpful comments.

COLLOQUIUM 4

Commentary on Ewegen

J.M. Forte
Northeast Catholic College

Abstract

This commentary begins by analyzing two textual selections about death in the *Gorgias* (486a7–b4 and 526e4–527a4) in order to expand upon Ewegen's portrayal of Socrates. I close by briefly giving voice to another, perhaps more familiar side of Socrates' rhetorical approach in the dialogue in order to provide some further perspective about Ewegen's claims.

Keywords

Plato – afterlife myth – Callicles – power – noble death

Ewegen's paper has provoked me to think about the *Gorgias*, as well as Socrates' death, in new ways. In order to explain this, I would like to turn first to one of Ewegen's textual selections and examine it in further detail. Callicles, in his assessment of Socrates' way of life, predicts Socrates' harsh demise:

> For now, if someone seized you or anybody else ... and carried you off to prison, claiming that you were doing an injustice when you were not, you know that you would not have anything of use to do for yourself, but you would be dizzy and gaping, without anything to say; and when you stood up in the law court, happening to face a very lowly and vicious accuser, you would die, if he wished to demand the death penalty for you. (486a7–b4)[1]

Plato, in his portrayal of Callicles' foretelling, directs the reader to conclude that Callicles' assessment of Socrates' fate is correct in a way. Socrates will

---

1   Translations from the *Gorgias* are by James H. Nichols Jr.

114   FORTE

die unjustly at the hands of accusers who are "lowly and vicious" (φαύλου καὶ μοχθηροῦ, 486b3).[2] He will be powerless to save himself.

Socrates does not correct Callicles. Rather, he responds by saying that he has found the best way to care for his soul, and implies that he will continue to do that (486d). Socrates speaks similarly in the *Apology*, saying that when one is doing what is best, one must remain there and continue to do so, even risking life and limb (28d–e). Here, in these lines of the *Gorgias*, I contend, following Ewegen's lead, that Plato directs the reader to the ultimate expression of the practice of philosophy—the art that takes men and makes them physically worse, as Callicles indicates—the art that denigrates their physical substance. The ultimate expression of the practice of philosophy, then, is to die as a philosopher. It is not only any death that characterizes a true philosopher. Rather, it is a death received from those who are "lowly and vicious." It is a death imposed by those whose assertions, arguments, and ways of life have been fodder for the philosopher's practice throughout his life. The philosopher receives death just as he receives opposition throughout life—by acknowledging and absorbing the truth of it—even if that truth is part of a caustic or poisonous mixture.

This is what Socrates does in the quotation above—he receives Callicles' argument, including the harsh truths mixed with his faulty position. The one who practices philosophy does not, then, respond as a sophistic rhetor—a man of power—does, with popular opinion or selfish interest as one's touchstone. Rather, the philosopher responds with truth as his only touchstone, "the best such stone" (486d4), as Socrates says in the lines just following the above text. The philosopher, when responding to interlocutors in the language of a soul with truth as *the* point of reference, has the tendency to confound those whose touchstone is the mere appearance of truth. The ultimate way in which the philosopher confounds his audience, then, is by letting himself die a noble death—ignoble if popular opinion is his touchstone, but fine and beautiful if that touchstone is truth. In this way, then, Ewegen's line of thought sheds new light on philosophy as practice for dying. The Socratic death, it can be argued, is the ultimate retreat, or self-effacement, to use Ewegen's terminology, that gives birth to the λόγος.

I would now briefly like to draw our attention to the closing myth, which Ewegen mentions toward the end of his paper. In the *Gorgias*'s myth of the afterlife (523a–527a), the powerful not only receive the harshest punishments (525c–d), but are Socrates' prime example of those whose souls are scarred and

---

2   All Greek references are to Burnet's Oxford edition.

COMMENTARY ON EWEGEN

deformed from living unjustly (See especially 525d–526b).[3] In that mythical rational account, it is the powerful who are least capable of caring for their souls in life, and who are therefore the most vulnerable after the separation of their souls from their bodies.

After describing the way in which souls are tried naked and then either punished or rewarded (523c–526d), Socrates turns Callicles' argument above on its head, saying:

> I reproach you that you will not be able to help yourself, when you have the judgment and the trial of which I was speaking just now; but when you have come to that judge … and when that one seizes you and brings you in, you will be gaping and dizzy there no less than I here, and perhaps someone will dishonorably strike you a crack on the jaw and completely trample you in the mud. (526e4–527a4)

According to Socrates, those who are the standard bearers of Calliclean values—the will to power, popular opinion, self-interest—are vulnerable to the sort of vicious denigration Callicles predicts for Socrates, but in a more severe way. Socrates does not go as far as predicting Callicles' psychic death, though the latter foresaw Socrates' bodily death, but the afterlife punishment Socrates describes is more permanent than bodily death. It is a fate suffered either indefinitely or for as long as it takes for one's soul to recover from the denigration and deformation self-imposed on one's immaterial substance. This mythical rational account could be interpreted both literally and metaphorically, as I have argued elsewhere.[4] Literally, the consequence for allowing one's soul to fester with injustice involves having those offenses exposed, and then either suffering fitting purgations until one is cured, or being flung into an underworld pit of torment for eternity. Metaphorically, one could argue that

---

3 The question of what the soul is in the *Gorgias* is worth addressing, at least briefly. Benardete 1991 explains that the "soul is simply the soul as rhetoric and morality have conceived of it, a metaphorical extension of body with a life of its own" (100). I do not completely agree with this, but it is a view worth considering, since there is no substantive argument for the nature of the soul in the *Gorgias*. I do contend that an immortal soul is at least implied in the dialogue, for instance in the closing myth.

4 Forte 2016, 187–208. Notable metaphorical readings of the myth: Edmonds 2004, 166; Ferrari 2012, 69; Fussi 2001, 535; Grosso 1971, 75; Guthrie 1975, 307; Hirsch 1971, 312; Emmanuel Levinas, according to Stähler 2008, 73; Rowe 2012, 193; Sedley 2009, 53; Stöcklein 1937, 11, 22–28. Others, like myself, who explicitly consider a metaphorical reading alongside a figurative one: Hitchcock 1974, 129–130; Olympiodorus, *Commentary on Plato's Gorgias*, 46.3, 46.4; and Russell 2001, 559–564.

Callicles' way of life necessitates eventually being exposed—perhaps to oneself, perhaps to others—and the result of such exposure will be some sort of suffering, which may be very long-term. Either way, those who opt for a life like Callicles' will suffer psychic torments, and will be humbled or reduced in both material and immaterial status. They will lose the physical substance they treasure most highly—fine clothes, status, wealth, and so on—*and* will also have their psychic substance, which they have allowed to be ruined, face the truth of its future. This does not, however, end in a death for the soul—let alone a noble one. The noble death is an empowering dignity that the philosopher gets, to follow Ewegen's line of thought and combine it with my own. This of course implies the indestructability of the soul, and is part of Socrates' thesis that the good person cannot be harmed in life or death (527d). The one who seems least powerful then, actually possesses the greatest power according to the dialogue, expressed in its final myth: the power of invincibility in the face of the ultimate contest—the one in which the victory of the soul is at stake.

Though it is clear that I largely agree with Ewegen's line of thinking, I will end here by suggesting that we give voice to another side of this account: Socrates' positive attempt to persuade his audience. On the one hand, though Socrates does advance his position, paradoxically, by retreat and self-effacement, on the other, he also advances arguments in attempts to persuade his audience. In other words, his approach to his interlocutors is not completely portrayed by his receptive posture. He may even make use of rhetorical tricks in advancing his arguments.[5] The fact that those who argue for the latter largely claim that they are *ad hominem* attacks leaves open the possibility that any of Socrates' positive attempts to persuade are done for the sake of the souls of his audience—so if he is portrayed as arguing against the person, it could be simply because he is doing it *for* the person, and not because he sees such techniques as the best way to advance λόγοι. Furthermore, many of the conclusions for which he argues are incredibly unique and compelling. They have the distinct "brand" of Socrates. Even if his efforts are more about promoting the λόγοι than himself, he is quite present in those λόγοι as their champion. But it is not the purpose of Ewegen's paper, as I understand it, or my comments, to add to the vast body of scholarship on Socrates' hypotheses in the *Gorgias*, or the possibility that he advances these using techniques that bear similarity in some ways to the very rhetoric he criticizes. Rather, my comments here are meant to echo Ewegen's portrayal of an underappreciated aspect of the complex

---

5   Three notables who argue that Socrates commits fallacies are Kahn 1983, 75–121 (all three of Socrates' arguments are *ad hominem*), McTigue 1984, 193–236 (Socrates commits *ad hominem* against Polus), and Vlastos 1967, 454–460.

COMMENTARY ON EWEGEN

character that is Socrates in the *Gorgias*: a figure who confounds his audience and advances the λόγος by means of withdrawal, receptivity, and an acceptance of the diminution of his wealth and social standing even to the point of physical death.

COLLOQUIUM 4

Ewegen/Forte Bibliography

Arieti, J., and R. Barrus, tr. 2007. *Plato, Gorgias*. Newburyport: Focus Publishing.

Benardete, S. 1991. *The Rhetoric of Morality and Philosophy: Plato's Gorgias and Phaedrus*. Chicago: University of Chicago Press.

Bianchi, E. 2006. Receptacle/Chōra: Figuring the Errant Feminine in Plato's *Timaeus*. *Hypatia* 21.4: 124–146.

Bourgault, S. 2014. The Unbridled Tongue: Plato, *Parrhesia*, and Philosophy. *Interpretation: A Journal of Political Philosophy* 41.2/3:65–90.

Burnet, J., ed. 1903. *Platonis opera*. Vol. 3. Oxford: Oxford University Press.

Edmonds, R. 2004. *Myths of the Underworld Journey*. Cambridge: Cambridge University Press.

Ferrari, G.R.F. 2012. The Freedom of Platonic Myth. In *Plato and Myth*, eds. C. Collobert, P. Destrée, and F. Gonzalez, 67–86. Leiden: Brill.

Forte, J.M. 2016. Turning the Whole Soul: Platonic Myths of the Afterlife and Their Psychagogic Function, Ph.D. diss. The Catholic University of America.

Foucault, M. 2005. *Hermeneutics of the Subject*. New York: Picador.

Fussi, A. 2001. The Myth of the Last Judgment in the 'Gorgias.' *The Review of Metaphysics* 54: 529–552.

Grosso, M. 1971. Death and the Myth of the True Earth in Plato's *Phaedo*. Ph. D. diss. Columbia University.

Grube, G.M.A., tr. 1997. *Plato, Apology*. In *Plato. Complete Works*, ed. J.M. Cooper, 17–36. Indianapolis: Hackett.

Guthrie, W.K.C. 1975. *A History of Greek Philosophy*. Vol. 4. Cambridge: Cambridge University Press.

Haden, J. 1992. Two Types of Power in Plato's *Gorgias*. *The Classical Journal* 8.4: 313–326.

Hirsch, W. 1971. *Platons Weg Zum Mythos*. Berlin: de Gruyter.

Hitchcock, D. 1974. The Role of Myth and its Relation to Rational Argument in Plato's Dialogues. Ph.D. diss., Claremont Graduate School.

Jackson, R., K. Lycos, and H. Tarrant, tr. 1998. *Olympiodorus, Commentary on Plato's Gorgias*. Leiden: Brill.

Kahn, C. 1983. Drama and Dialectic in Plato's *Gorgias*. *Oxford Studies in Ancient Philosophy* 1:75–121.

Lamb, W.R.M., tr. 1925. *Plato, Gorgias*. Cambridge: Cambridge University Press.

McCoy, M. 2008. *Plato on the Rhetoric of Philosophers and Sophists*. Cambridge: Cambridge University Press.

McTigue, K. 1984. Socrates on Desire for the Good and the Involuntariness of Wrongdoing: *Gorgias* 466a–468e. *Phronesis* 29: 193–236.

Nichols, J.H., Jr., tr. 1998. *Plato, Gorgias*. Ithaca: Cornell University Press.

Race, W. 1979. Shame in Plato's *Gorgias*. *The Classical Journal* 74: 197–202.

Rosen, S. 2008. *Plato's Republic: a Study*. New Haven: Yale University Press.

Rowe, C. 2012. The Status of the Myth in the *Gorgias*, or: Taking Plato Seriously. In *Plato and Myth*, eds. C. Collobert, P. Destrée, and F. Gonzalez, 187–198. Leiden: Brill.

Russell, D. 2001. Misunderstanding the Myth in the *Gorgias*. *Southern Journal of Philosophy* 39: 557–573.

Sallis, J. 1999. *Chorology*. Indiana: Indiana University Press.

Saxonhouse, A. 1983. An Unspoken Theme in Plato's *Gorgias*: War. *Interpretation: A Journal of Political Philosophy* 11: 139–170.

Schlosser, J. 2014. *What Would Socrates Do?* Cambridge: Cambridge University Press.

Sedley, D. 2009. Myth, Punishment, and Politics in the *Gorgias*. In *Plato's Myths*, ed. C. Partenie, 51–76. Cambridge: Cambridge University Press.

Stähler, T. 2008. Getting Under the Skin: Platonic Myths in Levinas. In *Levinas and the Ancients*, ed. B. Schroeder and S. Benso, 62–78. Bloomington: Indiana University Press.

Stöcklein, P. 1937. *Über Die Philosophische Bedeutung vons Platons Mythen*. Leipzig: Dieterich.

Strauss, L. 2004. "Plato's *Gorgias*." Published online at: <https://leostrausscenter.uchicago.edu/sites/default/files/Plato%27s%20Gorgias%201963.pdf>.

Vlastos, G. 1967. Was Polus Refuted? *The American Journal of Philology* 88: 454–460.

Zuckert, C. 2009. *Plato's Philosophers: The Coherence of the Dialogues*. Chicago: University of Chicago Press.

Index of Names

Alexander of Aphrodisias   63
Aristotle   2, 9n13, 26, 31–94
Augustine   58, 65

Barnes, Jonathan   39, 40, 47n8, 50n12, 78n15, 79, 81

Carroll, Lewis   82

Donini, Pierluigi   73, 74n7

Epimenides   16n20, 24
Euripides   83, 84

Foucault, Michel   104–106

Graham, Daniel   18, 19

Hardy, J.   79, 80n19–20
Homer   10, 75
Hume, David   40, 41

Janko, Richard   70, 77n11, 78n15, 79, 81, 82, 86

Malink, Marco   64

Melissus   8

Parmenides   1–30, 66
Patterson, Richard   64
Philoponus   63
Plato   17n22, 26, 34, 66, 73n4, 74, 91, 92, 95–119
Popper, Karl   18, 19n28
Priest, Graham   33

Rosetti, Livio   18, 19n26
Russell, Bertrand   40

Schmitt, Arbogast   77n12, 79
Sextus Empiricus   3, 24n5
Shakespeare, William   83, 84
Sisko, John   18, 22n2, 25
Sophocles   81, 89

Vecchio, Daniel James   64

Wittgenstein, Ludwig   24, 33, 40

Zeuxis   70, 71, 88

Printed in the United States
By Bookmasters